Praise for

MW00988901

"*Exquisitely considered and built out with one impeccably gorgeous sentence after another, Rifkin's stories are as honest and fully, soulfully inhabited as I remember them being when I first read (envied, studied!) him in magazines. As journalism continues to change and favor the hot take and fast draw, this is the kind of writing I miss most of all—larky and searching, yet meaningful and often mind-blowing. Surprise yourself and dive in.*"

    —Hank Stuever, *Washington Post* TV critic and author
       of *Tinsel* and *Off Ramp*

"*One of the true LA originals, Alan Rifkin is easy to catch in the act of being brilliant. He writes with a diamond cutter's artistry about everything from swimming pools to swooning hearts and knows that 'there's as much ache as joy' in both. There are only a handful of writers who can make anything interesting, and whether he's dealing with monks, dolphins, telescopes or unhappy marriage,* Burdens by Water *proves that Rifkin is one of them.*"

    —John Powers, Critic-at-Large, NPR's *Fresh Air*

"*Anything Alan Rifkin writes, I will read. Engaging, full of curious facts, often hilarious, and effortlessly profound, these essays zero in on the souls of their subjects, be they novice monks, neurotic writers, or a 5000 year-old mummy. Modesty, frankness and intelligence are Rifkin's trademarks—and oh, such beautiful writing.*"

    —Michelle Huneven, author of *Blame* and *Off Course*

"*Alan Rifkin's memoir takes us to wild places: from a Capuchin monastery and a Chilean observatory to the San Fernando Valley and the personal past. Alive with deep comedy, honesty and grace, this is a terrific book.*"

    —Charlie Haas, author of *The Enthusiast*

BURDENS BY WATER

AN UNINTENDED MEMOIR

Alan Rifkin

Brown Paper Press
Long Beach, CA

BROWN
PAPER
PRESS

Brown Paper Press
6475 E. Pacific Highway, #329
Long Beach, CA 90803

Cover by DR.ME
Interior by Gary A. Rosenberg

Image, page 73: Edward Biberman, Sepulveda Dam
Printed by permission of the Edward Biberman Estate,
courtesy Suzanne W. Zada, Gallery Z, Beverly Hills, CA.

Library of Congress Control Number: 2015954709

ISBN: 978-1-941932-04-9

10 9 8 7 6 5 4 3 2 1

Versions of "Boys in the Hoods," "Swimming with Dolphins," and "Thin Ice" appeared in *Details* magazine. Versions of "Pool Man," "The Metaphysics of Painting," "Measure the Universe," and "The Los Angeles Writing Club" appeared in *LA Weekly*. Versions of "The Metaphysics of Hang Time" and "Wave Theory" appeared in *LA Style* magazine. A version of "Consider the Richardsons" appeared in *Image: A Journal of the Arts and Religion*. A version of "E Luxo So (It's Only Luxury)" appeared in *Black Clock*. A version of "Requesting the Toronado" appeared in *California* magazine. A version of "Writing in the Dust" appeared in *The Los Angeles Times Magazine*.

To the memory of Herbert Rifkin, Phyllis Rifkin,
Susan Rifkin, and Bob LaBrasca

Contents

Wave Theory: A Prologue

Somewhere toward the end of a yearlong struggle to quiet our upstairs neighbor, the lead singer of The Nymphs, my then-girlfriend brought home an electronic noise-buster. This was the industrious girlfriend—a clever shopper and a determined person besides. Once, during her sleep, she snapped all the covers over her head and announced (her exact words): "You have to be crafty to pass Spanish One." She opened the new carton with a gleam.

But the project was only half successful. There were three dial settings on the noise-buster, each a thin wall of static. "Waterfall" was a roar. "Rain" was a hiss. "Ocean"—the setting she chose—alternated between the two, impossibly symmetrical, bereft of conviction, like an audition in a foreign tongue (Roar? Hiss? Roar? Hiss?), and it made me want to kill myself. It was a fine simulation of how waves sound, on planets that are shaped like cubes. Sue, for the record, slept like a castaway. She was from Knoxville, Tennessee.

I am from the San Fernando Valley, and I'm partial to the real rhythm of waves. Just how partial impresses me, because I'm rarely in the water anymore. A couple of things explain the depth of the memory. First, waves are worth remembering, a healing sort of memory. Second, it's hard to forget the motion of water after being overpowered by it six or eight hours a day, seven days a week, three or four summers running, a level of plain repetition that I think goes to the heart of the healing, though maybe only if you need as much healing as I do.

I remember those summers as a kind of campaign: The water so constant an opponent it invaded your sleep (try holding the bed still after eight hours of bodysurfing). And the evenings were an odd lull, a remission in the progress of a bout. Until finally the ocean displaced everything you could think of that wasn't the ocean.

Which is not a bad bargain: salty lips/nappy leg hair as the cost of clearing your head of foolishness. The only other things that have talked sense to me that way since are meditation and very strong sex. But at some level of abandonment the exact method is irrelevant, which is why everyone interchanges metaphors about all three.

My own most intense summers coincided with a presexual view of the world. When I was fourteen, only one guy in our crowd—bowlegged Bobby Weiser, small but imperially tough, tossing car keys to himself barefooted on the oil-spotted garage floor—had a girlfriend. The romance was all of ours, by proxy: They were our royal couple. And Weiser, too, was inexperienced, though this gave the relationship its air of teenage heroism. Once, Marie's bathing suit slipped in the crash of a wave, exposing one sad drenched nipple, and more than an hour later, she still had her face in her hands and was leaning against Weiser, who was whispering, "Nobody saw." I'd never seen my parents treat each other like that.

It was always the two of them out front, four shoulders under Weiser's towel, leading us down the bluff on the illegal path, dirt-caked feet kicking pebbles to the highway. Below, the ocean loomed like ill fate—because of our own sense of melodrama, the fear of battle, and the ritual of the long approach. I liked the buildup. I dreamed fright movies of the unwarm morning air, the fog near the coast, the light, bluer and more grim than Valley light, on the Santa Monica Freeway to Pacific Coast Highway.

The cure for all this apprehension, of course, was the ocean itself. And there are many ways to describe the education imparted by waves, but the one that leaps to mind is that they were a big pounding threat at the beginning of the day and a whitewater joke at the end of it, their pratfall and yours together; they left you stupid and reeling, with the low five-o'clock sun blasting the whiteheads, and seagulls descending, and all of us hungry, weak, and buzzed, and the beach empty of anyone older.

Is it redundant to think of waves as a series? First you have to wait for a set. And then swim out to the last wave of the set, which is the biggest. There are legends about the ninth waves of sets, and bigger legends about ninth waves of ninth sets, all diffracting in an infinity of excuses to stay in the water: Forever you run at one more wave. The far-off ones seem to build in slow motion, manufactured behind smaller decoys, haughty and monumentally steep, still adding inches and teeming at the crest and seemingly unreachable across a sudden expanse. And more or less wildly you charge the face, elbows high, scooping water with both hands for traction, finally to be swept upward, swimming hard out in front of the curl, eyes fixed downward to take you through the drop. Rocketing forward then. Scattering small kids in inner tubes.

Recovering, laughing, pulling up trunks in the shallow playground where the backwater crashes like cymbals against baby waves. Trudge back out, hug your own goosebumped arms, and wait for the next visitation/mirage.

The object, in a weird way, was self-forgetting. And in that department I may have been a specialist: Just as the rest of the gang played at adulthood (with pecking orders and anatomical jokes, loving the transparency of our own posturings), I was, in many ways, a pretender to the group: clearly the shyest and smallest—and so nicknamed, for the entire summer of 1969, "The Instigator." (A firecracker explodes in a trashcan, and a half-dozen fingers point at me.) I didn't kid myself about being a leader, nor did I mind being awed by tall waves. Or even just good waves. Two days stand out. There was the Perfect Day in Newport Beach that my friend Scott insists cannot be described except by a two-panel cartoon, the first panel showing two guys in a wave, and in the second panel they've carved a groove back to their towels, hands still tented an arm's length before them. And there was this one awful pilgrimage to the Wedge, just the name of which had me all but paralyzed on the trip down, a place where storm tides push against a jetty and form ten- or twenty-foot waves that break in waist-deep water. I pulled out of every single wave before it broke, to my lasting disgrace—a debacle that, in retrospect, segued directly to a different kind of high-school career entirely: one of false courage and cigarettes and beer, and scoffing at the whole world of genuine effort and risk.

There were more summers of driving to Santa Monica, but none with the same strange safety of fourteen. The glow gave way to age, and to a certain sexual materialism that's never been entirely escapable since. Jeff Rhodes showed up the next summer with a girlfriend of his own, an incomprehensible acquisition: a half-foot taller than he was, and lithe, and with the first ankle bracelet ever. I became a stealthy watcher of a girl in a lace bikini with peach fuzz on the backs of her legs, and I smoked cigarettes instead of finding a way to say hello to somebody who looked so complete without clothes. And I remember consciously deciding that if my face were tan enough, I would be invulnerable; I rotated my towel with the angle of the sun, and for years after had a self-conscious, front-only tan. Weiser went on to UCLA, and pretty soon all of us had summer jobs. Mine was at night, and I tanned in the daytime, wondering if I was having a good summer.

Gradually the beach became a thing for me to use, a compartment in a life with other goals. It would be a good place to dream of owning a house, or to take my wife for dinner—there were going to be multiple marriages in my future—or to drive by. It was, in other words, a backdrop for human plans, instead of a reminder of what's real, a reminder of why some plans are worth having while others are unbelievably foolish.

But I still know what the ocean sounds like; I'll never program a noise-buster to turn it into Muzak. And I believe an eight-hour swim could probably heal me. If I let it. The dangers are so different nowadays: that the waves will seem smaller than they used to, and that my life will seem bigger than the ocean. And then I'll have missed the lesson absolutely.

1

Boys in the Hoods

After a long day of prayer, what's on? Too many crime shows. *Top Cops! America's Most Wanted! Hard Copy!* An announcer growls out the name of whichever, and on comes tape of Ginger Lynn, the porn star, happily reunited with her mom after an unjust arrest.

In the TV room, the brown-hooded novices of the San Lorenzo Capuchin Friary sit watching in loyal decadence. They like to mimic the voice-overs and holler at the screen for more dirt.

"Wasn't that on *last* week?" Brother Bob asks, one knee crossed, flapping his sandal. "Didn't she get out of jail last week?"

Brother John says, "Maybe it's a follow-up interview."

"A startling new development," another novice says.

The notion cracks Bob up. "Story's been dragging on for *weeks!*" he declares. He takes a handful of Cheez-Its from a paper bowl.

Brother Jesus, waiting to defend the program at the perfect antagonistic moment, fingers his mustache, never turning his gaze from the set. He looks like a flyweight hearing prefight instructions. *"Hard Copy,"* he explains calmly, "happens to be one of the worthier shows on television. Like *60 Minutes* in half the time."

"For some reason I'm not sure that makes it better," Bob says.

"It's the number-one rated show in America."

"That I'm *sure* doesn't make it better."

"Are we talking about *facts?*" Jesus kicks back in his chair triumphantly. "Where's your *facts?*"

Bob ignores Jesus, and the other novice friars start to slip off toward their rooms, robes chafing.

It is pretty dark where they're going. One concrete corridor with a plaster statue of the Virgin Mary zigzags to the novices' wing, where a plaster statue of St. Anthony holds a solitary nightlight in the form of a candle. With communal hour ending, this light through a window may be the only visible glow for twenty-eight acres, aside from a great many stars. Subliminal in the dark are the Santa Ynez Mountains, camel-backed and bony and unusually green just now on account of recent rains. In normal months, they're chaparral and so parched that last year's novices accidentally touched off a brush fire.

The buildings are 1960s suburban barracks. At the end of a bluff, a wooden bench overlooks a neighboring ranch, where a few horses in a pen poke along, turning a millstone. In front of the bench, a cross made of four-by-fours is planted in a wash bucket of rocks. It's a big contemplative spot: alone on the cliff where, if a monk has taken one step after another to get away from the sound of his head, somewhere around here it's all supposed to die down, more or less of embarrassment, so he can see what's really around him.

TV seems silly at the monastery, yet necessary. After the novices take their first vows kneeling in the chapel, they will be free to watch as much TV as they want, and by then, they may not even want to. They will be all the way in. *Status perfectionis.* Right now, it's an hour a night, and the hour goes fast. Jesus is still hassling Bob when the credits roll. "Facts, dude! Give me facts!" He swaggers down the hall in his robe, the way he maybe once used to in street clothes, a parody.

Oneness, God, the jackpot. The storming of heaven. The goal is to cash in everything for the one greater thing, the thing that, if it existed and everyone knew it existed, no one would hesitate to trust it and to do the most absurd, radical deeds in its honor: stumble around in robes, hug lepers ecstatically, and shout praises under the stars.

But if it turns out that the call is an illusion, then the novice has been a sort of fool. He has been a fool either way, but while he's happy, it doesn't matter. The minute foolishness matters, you're marooned. The cross is just a cross, the Eucharist is just a chunk of bread, and there you pray, as the poet Amiri Baraka once put it, into your own cupped hands.

Brother Bob looks like he prays in quick muttered spurts. He's thickly set, with wavy brown hair and a beard, and when the subject of posing for magazine photos comes up, he shouts out, "We gotta lose weight!" At thirty-five, he's the oldest novice. This is to say that he stayed worldly the longest. He kept a stash of reporter's notepads from the *Santa Clara American,* where he used to work—he gives me one, a vaguely scary torch-passing, as if to say the monastery swallows writers.

Bob wasn't a convert, just a sort of a holdout—philosophy student at San Francisco State, deep thinker in pubs—a posture that defined his theology. "I liked the idea that you couldn't hide from God. You could run from women or jobs, but not from God."

Whether he had a lifelong calling to the priesthood was another question, made harder by the fact that his invitation from God had lacked some traditional wallop. In the Book of Acts, St. Paul was knocked to the ground by a Light from the Sky; Bob just saw a recruitment poster (depicting a Franciscan priest pointing out a sunset to a waif) and mailed in the free postcard for further info. Other guys crumpled to their knees over something or other on a printed page: Brother Jesus had read Paul's second letter to Timothy and felt "all of God's joy and sorrow for the world." Brother Anselmo, having prayed for guidance while on retreat, opened a textbook after midnight to the lines, "Let me cure all your wounds of selfishness and pride. Come to me. Don't be afraid," and that pretty much did it. He ran deliriously to the end of a corridor and stood

whanging on a door to tell a groggy elder: "Father Miguel—
I want to be a Capuchin!"

Whereas Bob had seemed to follow a line of utterly
unmagical curiosity—pulling a single dark thread inch by
inch and watching his proudest sport coat unravel. "I guess
I was motivated by some idea of truth," he says. "Which
meant I had an obligation to consider anything." When the
issue didn't go away, he assigned it a gambler's contingency.
If he hadn't made it by age thirty as either a musician or a
reporter at a big-city newspaper, he was going to investigate
joining the order.

As it turned out, he stretched the deadline to thirty-two.
He was hanging on at the newspaper until the day he called
the publisher a son of a bitch in a fight over salary. It seemed
clear, too, that he hadn't made it as a jazz guitarist—he'd
been fooling around in a country band, drinking Bass Ale
and plucking at a Les Paul. He stepped outside the newspaper office feeling all Earth's gravity and more, knowing what
came next, with the thought *I don't want to do this* trailing
him in doomed soprano. Demons battled for his soul. ("The
devil's finest triumph," according to one novitiate manual, is
"the undoing of a vocation.")

Everything but the calling started to look like a calling.
The Fabulous Baker Boys—Jeff and Beau Bridges playing
greasy cocktail music in tuxedoes, Michelle Pfeiffer snaking
her way across a polished Steinway—looked very much like
a calling.

After one year of postulancy (he taught homeless addicts
in San Francisco to read) and the better part of a year at

San Lorenzo, he still wasn't sure of anything, though it could be argued he wasn't supposed to be. Father Enda, the novice master—a white-haired extrovert with the inevitable brogue, a canvas windbreaker over his robe—liked to define the novitiate as a courtship. "You're engaged to the girl, but you're not married to her yet."

Late at night, though, the stakes filled both sides with holy terror. The "greater number" of damned souls, according to St. Alphonsus, were damned by "not having corresponded to their vocation." No elder wanted to steer anyone to damnation by vocational error—and possibly be dragged down as an accomplice—but every three months a panel of them had to vote on each candidate's future, fingers on the lever to Hell. One year, Enda asked three of eight novices to leave. One was judged too high-strung, another unable to let go his bitterness about a physical defect ("I personally felt he had a vocation," Enda says, "but the community didn't agree"), and the third got into contemplation so deep he became a silent Trappist, his portrait still gazing past horizons from the seminary kitchen wall.

To survive the final "votation" in June would be to march forward in Mystical Marriage to the taking of public vows (chastity, poverty, and obedience)—an event that religious texts describe, with almost carnal enthusiasm, as "personal holocaust." Burial veils used to be draped over the newly professed. St. Margaret Mary, on the eve of her ordination, opened a vein and wrote in her blood, "Margaret Mary, dead to the world." You either had a taste for this stuff or you didn't.

Then came assignment to a mission, either in Watts, Fresno, or Bend, Oregon—the hangover after the honeymoon. The dawning of irrevocability. "We know we're good guys or we wouldn't be here," Bob says. "It's the vows that are going to test us." He still owned three guitars, for example—no serious violation of the vow of poverty, but he was learning how attached to possessions he still was. Or maybe he was using attachment in order to stall. The consensus on Bob's most recent votation was: good fellowship, good sense of humor, but too intellectual, stringing out the whole question of commitment.

Brother Jesus at the same juncture was judged to have a problem with "smugness." Brother Bobby, who wears a bright poncho and chortles like a bandit, was admonished to cover his mouth when he yawned. Brother Mike, jerking a lawnmower across a hard hillside at dusk, was urged to examine his perfectionism.

I'm visiting these guys at a time when God can pick up any celebrity interview and read nice things about Himself from the mouths of gifted amateurs—Grammy winners, Olympic medalists, people who may never need to know any more about God than that they're not God, who stay high on the first free hit of self-forgiveness.

And what would God make of me? In my secular/Jewish Valley childhood, even the least religious Catholic school kids—flouting rules and popping cherries, all their sins tediously forgiven—looked alien and churchy in their Old World uniforms: The gated stone playground at St. Cyril's on Ventura looked like the kind of place where you'd accidentally bowl over Madeline while chasing a handball. Traditional religion seemed lost in the heart of the West Coast experiment.

But like every LA kid, I grew up knowing that there was More to Here Than Here. Something shimmered with revelation; something in the desert light attracted both seeker and huckster to the tent.

By the time I hit thirty, Higher Power mysticism had entered the vocabulary of almost everyone I knew in Hollywood. I'd just never asked how far the Godly obsession could take you—I'd never met anyone who loved God for a living. Except in the way everyone who loves their children loves God, and not counting old Rabbi Hirschberg at Temple Judea, whom I never imagined that vulnerable, because it would have been like kissing him on the lips.

Brother John is a big ex-marine with slick black hair. "Want some great trivia?" He pokes my elbow to show me a giant poster on the dining room wall. Above the words IT WAS NOT YOU WHO CHOSE ME, IT WAS I WHO CHOSE YOU, Christ's silhouette consoles a humbled youth. "The smaller figure," Brother John says, "is Gregory Peck. He was a Capuchin in Hollywood for a short time in the nineteen-thirties." Immediately John admits this to be a fantastic lie. He shrugs happily.

A true piece of trivia is that the Capuchin robe, if flattened out like a bear rug, unfolds into a cross. On the other hand, so would a bear rug. It's the pyramid hood that's distinctive, the result of a sixteenth-century holy dispute over how it was that St. Francis dressed exactly. Regular Franciscans kept wearing what they always had, but the new sticklers followed Matteo da Bascio, who'd grown a beard and was starting to go around barefoot.

Next the Capuchins elevated to a science the Franciscan balance between prayer and worldly works. The whole point of contemplating God was to fill up with light so you could then go pour it on lots and lots of people. Or this was how St. Francis had seen it. Drawn, always, in the shape of a lit candle, bluebird roosting on his sleeve, Francis of Assisi in 1219 was the kind of people-person who could stride unarmed in rags across a battlefield in Egypt, requesting an audience with the sultan—whom he would then win over in witty conversation. Granted, solitude could be romantic, too. But your soul had to be halfway perfected just to appreciate the thrill, and by the early 1960s, contemplative Cistercians were outnumbered eight to one by the less austere Franciscans, who also went to a movie now and then.

One movie that comes up at dinner is 1986's *The Name of the Rose* (Sean Connery/Christian Slater murder mystery set in a monastery). Father Enda recommends the film, and Brother Bobby says, "Yeah, but they made the monks look like total lunatics."

"Well, some of us are," Enda says.

And John says, "Yeah, but that one scene? Come on!"

"What scene?" Enda says.

John says Enda knows exactly what scene he means. At this Enda's face becomes a pinched sneeze. "Well, of

everything in the movie, tell me why all you're rememberin'
is this scene!"

John is on his feet clearing dishes, looking innocent.
"God made me this way!" he says. "I take no responsibility!"

In the scene, a novice has slow, mute, astonished sex with
a medieval Eve-waif, hair across her mouth, who hoists sex
up and out of him in a couple dozen pelvic stops and starts,
feeding from her hips. It's all bodies in robes and then in
open air, bodies asserting from robes, until the robes are a
dashed joke and the bodies have their eternal say. It's a hot
scene and in silence it seems to last forever.

Nobody pretends chastity isn't the killer vow. How much
so is hinted at by the martyred tenor of their instructions
for coping with it, namely turning deprivation itself into a
kind of partner, "entering loneliness," as one Capuchin manual puts it—an idea that, if you're a guy in your twenties,
could sound borderline lovely at times but also charade-like,
ready to end on the hour, like ballet class. Raymond Chandler defined the struggle for all time in the sentences, "It was
a blonde. A blonde to make a bishop kick a hole in a
stained-glass window." *This* rings a bell: the novices very
much suspect they've seen this blonde. They see blondes
like this almost every week in Santa Barbara on their free
day. And brethren elsewhere see her in the twilight state of
presleep, and climax into their sheets without sin, because,
as defined by the Church, volition is absent if the trance is
deep enough. Spiritual directors interrogate novices to get
at the truth.

All of which suffering offers the vague consolation that

the brothers are "normal" ("If they didn't get a little hyper around pretty girls," Enda says, "we'd have to send them home.") and that on the surface they may prove stronger than they think. "If God is calling you," Bob figures, "He'll give you sufficient grace to carry it through."—a measure by which nine out of ten Catholic priests who'd asked for dispensation in the previous year must not have had a calling, naming sexuality as their reason for wanting out.

No trouble right now for Brother John, who wipes plates in the kitchen after dinner and says he's in one of his better grooves with God while it lasts. "Sometimes in meditation," he says, "you just tell God, 'I'm here, and my mind is a million other places, but you made me this way, so this is it.' There's something to be gained in every struggle if you embrace it."

He's been looking all day like a guy who's solved a problem. Morning reading had been about Exile: souls in exile, Hebrews in exile, wandering hordes lost from themselves, as John himself may feel again tomorrow or the next morning. So I ask him why people can't feel ecstatic all the time, forever found. He says with the gleam of knowing everything for a second, "Because this isn't our home."

Tuesday before Ash Wednesday the novices go to some Capuchin meetings in Altadena, outside LA, but end the day in a royal screw-up. With heavy rain falling and freeways jammed at dusk, they stay for dinner in Altadena, taking a back route home through Simi Valley and asking Brother Matt, an adviser, if it's all right after the long drive to sleep through morning mass. Matt says he thinks so, but nobody tells Father Enda, who alone has the authority to decide. It's unclear whether the novices have prayed for God's perfect guidance when they already have in their pocket this unmistakably supportive verbal okay from Matt. At 7 a.m., Enda is chanting at the service, *Remember you are dust and to dust you shall return,* craning his neck in the pauses to watch for the young novices of San Lorenzo Seminary, who don't arrive.

"As a family, you start Lent together," Enda says angrily over cornflakes afterward, a medallion of ash stamped on his forehead. "I realize they asked Matt, but they shouldn't have done it."

Punishment is nothing outrageous—the novices have to forfeit their weekly free day in exchange for half a day off today—though even this ruling seems to bring up a certain ambivalence in Enda about discipline. His answer to confusion these days is to go with it. It shows he's a real guy. Used to drink too much, still hooked on cigarettes, but he's trying to cut down. In the same manner, he fusses with the novices. Three novices by his estimate are extroverts (Bobby, Jesus, and John), three are introverts (Bob, Mike, and Anthony), one uncertain (Anselmo), and his goal is to pull the inward guys out and the outward guys in, settling toward the golden mean.

"*I* haven't had a sleep-in day in two weeks," Enda tells several of the novices later. He says it into hushed nonresistance. "I may take one Friday."

The peace gets strained when the brothers are alone

later. Bob paces around the kitchen in his sandals and his logic switches on. "How he thinks we were trying to trick him—I don't get that. That's what pisses me off. I mean, if I wanted to get away with something, I wouldn't be hanging around here. I'd get out of here and get a free day out of it. I don't think any of us are here to play games."

Bobby keeps philosophical. "Look, I'm figuring, why should I even dwell on it? We had a good day." (With allowance up to seven dollars a week from last year's six, Bobby was able to see a play at a small theater in Solvang.) "I didn't mind the half day. If I don't mind, where's the problem?"

Brother Jesus's point exactly. "I don't got no guy with a gun to my head," he says. "Supposedly I wanted to be here." He stands in the doorway looking at mountains, willing to see paradise if it turns out this is it. The sun has partway returned, and some trees in the distance look smoky and veined. Rains have flooded the basketball court behind the stations of the cross, beyond which stand some grapefruit trees that Jesus is assigned to water—with a single garden hose to make the job harder, to make a meditation out of it. *Tree, grow,* he is supposed to think over and over, pulling the extrovert back in.

Lately, meditation has started to snowball for Brother Jesus. Now he's got meditations written on index cards. ONE WHO PRAYS IS SAVED, ONE WHO DOES NOT IS DAMNED. Brother Bobby saw that one and asked hesitantly, "Isn't that kind of . . . hard?"

Jesus just stares at the card, striking spiritual gold every time.

Last week with Lent approaching, Brother Jesus even volunteered to give up free days altogether, reading his index cards and answering phones with the infirmarian, Brother Joe, instead. He was walking on coals, showing the way, feeling no pain.

Silence brings its own greed. One day I feel harassed by a golf cart bumping along a meadow two hundred yards away.

Of course, my annoyance means I've already drifted from real quiet into something else, its own mirage, something ersatz and governable—a gated community, a silence of my own making. I am humbled to realize this. I have a perfect humble instant. This notices itself and turns into pride. The soul is a house of mirrors.

And up above, if you're religious, all kinds of fates hang on your private intentions and your public motions. You cut yourself, some ancient soul bleeds. If you're too modern for religion, the same thing happens figuratively, maybe in the conscience, where demons go by more bloodless names.

"We take a beating for this stuff," Bob says, "but it exists. It isn't metaphor. Evil exists. Satan exists."

"The devil exists, but he's overrated," Brother John says.

God exists on a radio band. Sometimes you're on His wavelength, sometimes not. "You just bring the body sometimes," Bob says. "Christ is always present anyways. I mean, God's omnipotent—*you're* the one who keeps forgetting. If I don't get this great glow all the time, so what? He's omnipotent! So what the hell?"

On the other hand, it seems unfair that souls can simply

drift off the base paths and get penalized, just when they're trying their hardest to stay the course. In fact, trying sometimes makes things worse. "When you're trying the hardest to do God's will," Bob says, "you're often the most insufferable guy on the planet." Yet given the eternal stakes, how can you not try?

"The church exists in heaven as well as on earth," Bob explains. "So we're all praying toward heaven, and the people there are praying for us." Back in college Bob decided it was as reasonable to believe in the mechanics of heaven as not to. It was still a lot to swallow. By the Angelic Salutation, God became a man, a virgin became the mother of God, the souls of the just were delivered from Limbo, and the empty thrones of heaven were filled. St. Dominic drove a hundred devils out of the body of a heretic; they pressed out in the form of hot coals. In 1917, on the day three children spotted the Virgin at Fatima, the sun took off spinning in the sky over the Vatican; forty years later Pope Pius XII confirmed he'd seen it happen.

Nor do religious vows, in the Catholic view, merely chasten one priest's soul. They atone for the sins of others. They balance the whole order of goods. That is why bands of Franciscans crossed the Southwest in the 1930s half nude, carrying 250-pound cross beams, monotonously lashing braided yucca whips over one shoulder first and then the other, falling on faces in the dirt. Calling God's hand, finding out what part of the self could not be destroyed. Believing finally the rest is just a decoy. That this new realm was the real one.

When he's lived awhile, in the world but not of it, a monk takes on a certain look. He looks spoken for, like he's right where he belongs. He looks this way when you see the outlines of the dream he sees around him. If you cannot see his dream, he can just look unreachable, creepily insistent, past the last stop. At San Lorenzo, the man at the outer reaches is Brother Joe, the infirmarian, a fixture of twenty years who offers me his story one night standing motionless in the darkened dining room at closing time, nowhere to sit, no coffee cup to hold. He looks exactly like he does in a news clipping I saw of him ringing the bells of Mission Santa Ynez (a lifelong dream fulfilled): impish, blissfully modest, as if he broke the laws of time in order to surface there. Normally he only smiles and performs small courtesies; this night he's decided to outdo himself. However squirmy I appear, he'll talk for as long as I let him. He's the keeper I might have pictured lurking behind those gates of St. Cyril's in my childhood.

Like Brother Bob, he had tried to escape his calling. As a sailor on Guam, he was moved by a profile of then–Sister Teresa in *Look*. He transferred to Mountain View, California, but some priests came recruiting there, too. He transferred back to Guam. He told God, as he would tell you or me, "You've got the wrong guy!" He promised himself he would stay away from anyone religious. A typhoon hit, destroying three-fourths of the island, so the base opened up to give aid and in came an army of nuns.

Brother Joe reports these phenomena, hands clasped and with a smile, not moving until I leave. He is the infirmarian for the order now, and he explains that he loves it, caring for aging priests throughout the West. Pretty often, he's the last thing they see before they die.

Enter loneliness. Stay or go. "I'm frightened of both answers," Bob says. "You're sort of out there flapping in the wind and wondering what you're going to be doing. All of my friends are married and buying houses. And I'm doing this. And if God says, 'Well, this is wrong—you've got to leave'. . . I'm going to have to have faith it's going to work out."

All the novices are sitting around talking about destinations—Bend, Fresno, and Watts. Watts is the scariest, and there's a perception it's been hard on the guys who've recently been assigned there. "Look at them!" one novice says. "I mean, a couple of these guys weren't even from cities—completely unprepared. They looked really bad when we saw them."

The description registers glumly on all the faces, and a few stay glum, but a few go past glum and just give it all up in exchange for gallows humor. Maybe the order will abandon the outpost in Watts. Maybe some of the novices will be sent there and not even know the order has abandoned the outpost in Watts. A bishop will visit in five years and Brother Bob will have it going as a blues bar. "And he won't say a damn thing, I tell ya," Bob says, "if we're pulling in the bucks!"

The others will have failed their votations. Graduation photos will show a pile of brown habits.

"But I'll be interviewed by a Catholic monthly," Bob says. "With those newsmaker headshots, you know, three stills of me talking. Big, fiery gestures! A hot dog in one hand and a beer in the other!" He can't stop laughing.

In the TV room, Maury Povich interviews Desi Arnaz, Jr. Another storm is up outside, skies black, wind hounding the trees.

Father Enda has turned sixty. Actually, he'll turn sixty on St. Patrick's Day, but he won't be home on that date so cake is served a week early. He has a slice at dinner and reminds the novices that breakfast should be silent all through Lent. Also he comments on the morning's Bible reading, in which God managed by heroic self-control not to smote the brazen Hebrews—an image I find terrifying, all the power of Heaven braced in battle against itself. But Enda hears the story differently. "It's about love," he says, wiping his mouth. "It's about God's patience."

Night prayers, 7:30. The seven novices and Father Enda all pray facing the altar, stained glass twinkling, no one facing back. Like toy passengers, no one driving. "Virgo Maria, Mother of Mercy, Queen of All Angels," on and on: the Virgin gets a hundred names. They pretty much chant until the walls fade.

They look estranged. They look as if it's their fault they can't disappear all the way and be with Jesus, looking down on themselves. They look apologetic about this trick they can never do.

They keep trying to work it out with God. Brother Mike works on his distrust. His problem is assuming that what's important to him is what's important to God. ("Why isn't God helping me finish the lawn by noon?") While he's thinking for God, he can't see God. Or he sees some God he created in his own image.

Brother Bob sees God and loses God and sees God again. He defends the voters who've critiqued him. "Maybe they just think I should be working on it. Because if I worked on it more with God, I'd get a clear answer. Either I'd become more committed or I'd pack my bags." I ask Bob how he's getting on with God right now, and he laughs: "Actually, pretty well."

Brother Jesus has had another breakthrough in meditation. He imagined himself being cradled by Jesus Christ. He felt almost perfected. He walked around grinning for a long time afterward. He felt sorry that in thirty minutes it had to end.

2

Swimming with Dolphins

BAHAMAS—VOLUNTEERS WANTED. Using only snorkel equipment, we will dive and glide with pods of free-swimming dolphins who seem to enjoy human companionship. Assist scientific researchers. No special skills or experience required.

Flipper was cute, but could he save the planet? To buy in required some personal ferment. In my case, I was fumbling to set a clock radio in the dark and wound up breaking up with a girlfriend.

She said, "The button is right there!"

"Right where?"

"For God's sake, let me sleep."

"I just need the light on for a second."

"Why are you doing this to me?"

"Why are you doing this to *me?*"

—while far away, I knew, dolphins peaceably, anciently, tossed. Maybe even a little sorrowfully. It was hard to tell.

The great genius of other sentient species—all but our own—is to bubble along at the periphery of strife: Civilization isn't their fault. This makes dolphins look even more sentient than they would otherwise, and a little smug, like Bruce Willis. I can pinpoint, to the month and year, all my past fixations with mystical animal quiet; they followed mighty attempts at communication with humans. For a few weeks in my twenties, my dream life was filled with images of amphibians—briefly, but with such intimate force that the whole fantasy seemed like a fresh, pink self inside a crusty old self, and it seemed to dart from the light, which came shining through a crack in a rock. This was in the dim of winter. I had tobacco-stained walls and a card table as a desk, and I felt cold from fear of feeling cold. My life felt like a bear suit.

Another time, I labeled a series of notebooks "Cetacia." They were aquamarine, and they contained fetishistic passages about an island girl who showered on shoals and whose hair was so wild you could hear it thicken in the steam.

In the months before the breakup, I saw *White Fang*—twice—a film I'd have shunned as a twelve-year-old, because I had no use at twelve for courage in the wild or for finding out who I really was down deep. Now I was reading both Thomas Merton and *The Call of the Wild,* hoping to meet God in the Very Ground of My Being. I don't know if I met God. Random encounters with dogs felt more poised on the brink of infinity than usual.

I remembered, too, getting a portentous nudge from my friend Jim Smith. A scrawny actor from Alabama who drove a post-hippie van, Jim was for me the quintessentially uncritical Angeleno. I had driven him to Cedars-Sinai Medical Center one time when he nearly died from appendicitis, and he bore the pain clutching a porkpie hat to his head, in a wordless embrace of destiny. Trying to make conversation that night, I asked him what he'd most like to write about if he were me. "Dolphins," he said—point blank, as if he were on truth serum. There were no thoughtful delays in him, ever.

One of the participants on the Expedition—there were eight of us—told me dolphins regularly spoke to her. In English, specifically, and not just in her dreams. An example of something they told her was "Stop creating money as a distraction." It makes the case for dolphin telepathy a little tidy, of course, that the things dolphins are quoted as saying are always the things you would tell yourself if you had the courage; in the presence of a willing-enough conscience, redwood trees speak pretty fair English, too. But I liked the personal-adviser angle. I had in mind a dolphin closer to me than I was to myself, what people would be without the curse of opposable thumbs: puppetlike, sublime, knowing all the eternal truths I knew in my cells but had managed to forget in my puzzling drive to amass atomic weaponry. And I could bolster this fantasy with facts. Brain size to body mass: Dolphins were highest. Abstract thinking: Dolphins had been taught, in a breakthrough experiment, not only a repertoire of tricks but a special *category* of trick that meant "invent a new trick." They could distinguish the genre from the particular. They were sanguine and gregarious, and, since 1847, they'd cooperated in a quid pro quo with Brazilian fishermen, herding mullet fish into nets for the privilege of feeding on the overflow.

On the plane to Florida—an emissary on behalf of Jim and all the dreamers of Hollywood, going to meet our sister species—I held to these truths like bouquets. If dolphins looked like they were winking cosmic reassurances to humans across eternity, it seemed good to believe that they were, and to wink back. Even if, when you looked closely, both sides turned out to be bluffing, and nobody knew anything really, and the dolphins were swimming straight into a cloud of sea lice, and the waters were laced with the usual doubt.

Night one. Sprawled about the deck, we squinted at a slide show of the regulars. Close-ups: smooth bodies, corona-like noses, drive-by grins. Group shots: puckered tails, traffic jams, a spilled shipment of cigars. "I'd like to know," said participant Dave, "do they identify us? Do they say, 'I know that gal from last year'?" Dave was a nice-guy jabberer from New Jersey, a heart patient, filling Dixie cups of wine on doctor's orders. His wife, Gail, was all gutsy good cheer, walking the tipsy deck like a talk-show host and tying thought-provoking ribbons at the ends of conversations.

"I think they do," answered the scientist, Pamela Byrnes. "And I've been in situations where common dolphins—I saw this many times, in the Sea of Cortes—will porpoise out of the water and actually turn in midair, tip, and look into the boat. It's as if they're saying, 'What kind of boat is this? Are these guys gonna harass us?' And with us, they decided to bow-ride along with the boat. I don't know if they would have decided any differently if we'd been standing there with big spears or something."

She clicked to the next slide. "Now, traditionally," Byrnes said, "to find out what a wild dolphin does, people have looked at the animals from this view." The view was from on deck, looking down. "But to find out how they live in their natural state, you really need to get out in the ocean."

That was a more sporting arrangement than my original plan. My original plan had been to get to know one dolphin in a pen. Slowly at first, evolving into fierce boyhood loyalty over time. It may never have worked, plus it required a captive dolphin, an inequity that might foster hidden resentments down the road. More than 50 percent of dolphins in captivity develop stomach ulcers, permafixed smiles notwithstanding—a statistic I'd been hearing repeatedly from activists in Florida, where the debate over captivity seemed to be entering extra innings. Conservationists printed up T-shirts showing a dolphin wearing a ball and chain. The president of a Fort Lauderdale theme park supplied the swelling testimony, "If I died and came back as dolphin, I'd want to be right here at Ocean World."

The environmentally correct way to swim with wild dolphins is passively, hands behind your back (wild dolphins "don't understand arms," the Oceanic Society told me), inconspicuously, *apologetically* if you can possibly manage it—a pantomime of underwater life. In glass-clear water at the shore of Grand Bahama island, Byrnes had run everyone through last-minute snorkel education, stressing peripheral vision. A snorkeler chugged along and Byrnes would play the dolphin, hovering just behind, right in the blind spot. "You just missed your encounter!" she'd triumph then, cracking air. We all futzed with our fogged masks, pondering excuses.

Somewhere the fear lurked: Could you really ruin an encounter—maybe all your encounters, one after another for eight days—by bad ocean etiquette, a thoughtlessly exposed forearm, poor rearview vision? It would seem like a shame, and not very charitable on the dolphins' part. I felt that rush of indignation in advance of rejection (we were children of the universe—we might be worth getting to know!). Simultaneously I consoled myself that the odds might be with us after all. Whereas previous expeditions included an eighty-year-old woman who couldn't swim, ours had no obvious liabilities. We had, by pure coincidence, two women with dolphin ankle tattoos. One was a Santa Barbara firefighter, and she swam underwater with a powerful dolphin kick, flinging ocean leagues behind her. The other was a Berkeley student from LA, leonine and completely ingenuous. (On meeting a participant from Hummelstown, Pennsylvania, she gasped: "There's really a city called Homeless Town?") And all of our brows were already blown vacant and gentle by the soft Bahamian unreality, so we were nicer than we normally would have been, which I think was nice to begin with.

Compared with dolphin niceness, of course, ours looked like a smudge on a turquoise glossy, and we knew it. The spotted dolphins of Little Bahama Bank, in particular—the species we'd be encountering—had seemed to glide uncorrupted through fate. In form and gesture they seemed so streamlined (one photo I saw of two calves touching pectoral fins together was as symbolic and symmetrical as a weathervane) that it was hard to remember they were animals and not, say, emblems. Once in a while, predators tore dime-sized bites from their sides and then fled, like vandals. With humans, the history had been split: no underwater contact for centuries, and then waves of playmates beginning in 1972, when treasure divers exploring a seventeenth-century Spanish galleon swam around with the dolphins on breaks.

Afterward came bands of scientists. And idealistic volunteers. To enter into the pact those two dolphins seemed to offer in the photo—pecs touching, wall-eyes cast backward at the camera, naked, like John and Yoko—that was the great Aquarian hope. You could lie there on deck and prophesize it: a global future, the dolphin-human community (as the New Age was calling it), a vision of amnesty and virginity (John and Yoko, again!); none of the old mistakes counted. Of course, you'd be making fresh, new mistakes in a short while. Though on the boat, drugged by the rhythm of the swells, that worry seemed absurdly remote, impossible to rouse, like a lost appendage.

Little Bahama Bank qualified as frontier for scientific purposes, too. Most earlier dolphin research had been on captives and stranded loners. Until lately, there hadn't been a counterpart to Dian Fossey's gorillas or Jane Goodall's chimps. Enter the spotted dolphins, a population of about 200, with their social order still intact. Eighty-six individual dolphins with names like Blaze and Macho and Zen had been photo-ID'd from an avalanche of snapshots. Byrnes now fantasized solving certain harder questions: Did the spotteds really time-share their turf with the bottlenose dolphins? Did they venture into hostile deep waters to feed? Did they use their echolocation (radarlike clickings and groanings) to stun their prey? This last was a burning mystery. It was generally agreed that dolphins *can* stun their prey (in a kind of deep sea Ella Fitzgerald-versus-Memorex experiment, tape recordings of echolocation had successfully zapped the daylights out of little fish); still, it was hard to get dolphins to use their special power. Attempts had gone like this: Scientist places fish in front of dolphin and sets up elaborate acoustical detectors; dolphin looks at fish and impressive equipment; dolphin eats fish.

Lastly, all eight of us might learn important things by living together in a contained environment. "You know, Pamela," remarked Gail, rising to speak, "something was touched on a little while ago about living together in a contained environment. Well, there was an article in the *New York Times* about a man who'd gone white-water rafting. And one thing resulted from that trip. He said he'd never really been able before to share certain parts of himself"— she cradled her solar plexus like a baby—"that he kinda kept inward. Well, on this rafting trip, he said that he truly opened up, and that was the most enriching part of his trip."

Byrnes nodded. "I see that a lot as trip leader. Because you're living in the moment; you're so there. The waves, the wind, the sun. You're just living life, and there's really a lot to say for that. Sometimes it brings you back to a feeling of 'Maybe this is what life is all about.'"

"It'll be interesting to see what's in it for all of us," Gail said.

That night, drifting to sleep, I was nearly "there" a couple of times—*there* meaning everywhere and nowhere, one with the big blue; living life, never getting in the way of my own encounter. And then I'd catch myself and hear my own thoughts and the rest of us talking, people on a boat in the middle of the ocean, poring over photos of the ocean.

The first two visits were false starts. High noon, nine hours from land, nothingness surrounding, nothing mattering finally, as if we'd severed the cord to Time.

From some seam at the back of all this stillness registered one tiny, distant leap. Just like that, an autograph, and then nothing—glassy turquoise. Seconds later, a closer, slightly larger charm bracelet of a leap, and someone screamed THEY'RE COMING TO THE BOAT! We piled into the water, torn between elbowing past each other and acting polite (what would the dolphins think of all our competitiveness?), but once underwater, we saw only each other and each other's cameras and each other's daffy fins strolling by. So we climbed back on board.

For what seemed like a long time I kept my mask on and stood dripping, looking along the deck now and then for somebody to tell me to relax. The water looked different now. The boat was oddly quiet. I panicked: The whole team was communing with dolphins on the other side of the boat, and they'd left me here. But that was just paranoia.

We made a next charge at empty water. Two silvery blurs, a mother and her calf, plain outraced four of us hydroplaning in a rubber Zodiac. But the mother whipped her tail at the calf, who doubled back to run rings around the raft, squibbing beneath like mercury shot from a tube. Byrnes killed the motor. "Let's get a couple of you in there."

"Here we go," Gail said. "Here we go to do the thing we all came to do."

Clumsy formalities, trying to get a body off a rubber boat and into water. We held our masks to our faces and rolled overboard, like corpses.

Bubbles cleared. The sandy bottom was maybe thirty feet down, a rippled dune. Human legs waved in the current, cameras dangling. No dolphins.

Back in the boat, nostrils filling with adventure, we relived the experience.

"Did you see the mother tail-kick that calf into line?" someone said.

"Pretty curious little guy," Brian said. Brian was a sandy-haired computer scientist from Silicon Valley.

"His mom put a stop to that, though!"

"They do that a lot, I understand."

"It's amazing they'd come anywhere near us at all, with the motor making that kind of racket."

"Well, not really," I said. "I mean, they probably know all about motors by now, and how close in is safe."

"Probably—yeah."

"They sure were in a hurry."

"Yeah. I think this is their feeding time. They prefer to play when they're done feeding."

Byrnes said, "Last year they came regularly in the mornings."

"Boy, they came right to the boat this afternoon, didn't they?"

"Well, they know the hull, what it sounds like, with their echolocation."

"I think they were just saying hi. And letting us know they were here, and that they'd be back later."

"Yeah—I think you're right."

By nightfall I felt almost pleased with the missed encounter. Something peculiar about group failure made it feel sheltering, intellectually manageable, like the Eisenhower years. We'd held up our end of the rendezvous, and now we could philosophize about it. Meanwhile, we could proclaim that, technically, we'd been open to new input all along. Thus we had short-circuited the unforeseen. But it was an ingrown, high-school sort of victory—it meant you didn't leave the dance with anything better than what you came with, ever—and I slept uneasily on my side with my back to the cabin, like the dolphins were all standing there waiting for me to stop being such an idiot. At 7 a.m., Gail called out, "Brian and Alan! You're missing the encounter!"

A narcoleptic stumble to the stern, ending in a peculiar protocol: fall in the water, search for your camera, then wake up. I dropped through some fishnets of foam and looked all around. I saw the rippled sand. A few small barracuda cruising low. A starfish. The hull of the boat. At the waterline I whipped my neck around, bewildered. New Jersey Dave was pointing from on deck: "The other side of the boat!"

When I got there, about eight flukes were slicing away like bats. The faster I swam, the farther away they got. Finally they vanished in the blue.

I puttered back to the ladder in disgrace. New Jersey Dave was pointing from on deck, smiling this time. "You've been followed," he said.

My strategy underwater was to Be Myself. There is a song by Suzanne Vega that goes, I think, "If you were to kill me now right here I would still look you in the eye." That approached the level of earnestness I was after. I dove down and glided around, wearing a facial expression that implied the sum of my life and everything I'd ever done, from the clock-radio incident on back. Immediately I sensed it beside me—the wide gleaming fuselage of an older spotted dolphin. I flanked him; he flanked me. I thought, *Here we are.* And I was more than willing to float there in place and resonate together as one, but the gap between us started to close in the current—I was about to bash into him! I freed one arm to straighten myself out, and he raced away.

I looked around underwater. No one had seemed to

notice the arm violation. There were other dolphins in small groups. At the surface, three of them cruised like a sidecar, veering and twirling in formation. At the bottom, two stood on their noses, taking turns pushing a shrub along the sand. I headed toward the twosome—competently, yet still capable of emotional vulnerability—but I couldn't get all the way down on account of ear pressure. It didn't matter. I was having a good time. I said it, through my snorkel: *We're having a good time!* I also said "chick-a-chick-a-chick-a" and "Here, dolphin!" The first noise brought one dolphin zoom-lensing to my face, eyeball to eyeball, scaring me to death; then that dolphin rolled over and swam away under the boat.

More bluish images, some chaotic, all surreal. Groups of dolphins surfacing for air in unison, stone-pony style. Long, baptismal, rhythmic sighs, a half-beat slower than your heart. At the outskirts of the action, people dangled, fins twitching, bodies strobed by reflected sun. Ending always in a smooth dolphin exit, taillights vanishing.

My first dolphin had been "TS," a female known by a deep gash on the tail stock. In the sonic, indecent heat we all rubbed our arms dry and compared notes. Some of us had seen more dolphins than others. (Estimates ranged between nine and twelve.) Some remembered everything, like intelligence agents, and others had gone brainless in the excitement. Some had cleared their ears well in the water and some had not, a subtle division forming. I had a foot in both camps—one day I couldn't clear, and the next day I could. Not that I was sure which group was the actual elite.

It was assumed, at first, that the dolphins preferred the deeper swimmers. But a backlash was forming, to the effect that the remedial people, who just drifted around on the surface, were actually getting the most dolphin *minutes*.

The trouble was that we kept swimming *at* dolphins, later to wonder if we'd really been *with* them, and then staring at the sea, which was blank and remembered nothing. When the dolphins did arrive—four times in the next twenty-four hours—they seemed strangely to have been there all along, or they just materialized, like ghost riders, double-exposing the water. "I think it's an illusion," I said. "When you go underwater, you're in the same place you were, but you're also someplace new, and your mind doesn't know how to handle that."

Lori the firefighter shrugged politely and held to her own theory, which centered on alpha waves: dolphins lived in an alpha state; when you were with them, you rejoined their strange frequency. This theory carried some weight, because Lori had had dolphin visions all her life—3-D flashes, eidetic as statuary, always sharper and closer than the scene you thought you'd been living in. She might be swimming at the Y; suddenly the lanes would be swarming with tailfins.

In any case, when you got out of the water—liquid, sapped, dazed—the whole experience would start to evaporate like the saltwater on your shoulders, and pretty soon you would just feel dry of it. And because dolphins were wonderful, you wanted to remember whatever truth it was that you felt in their presence. Which you couldn't put into words yet for alpha-wave reasons. But maybe later.

The desire to commune with dolphins could take on a certain me-first hysteria. Musical taste was a common battleground. An earlier expedition sank its hopes on playing a lot of Miami dance music and saw almost no dolphins for a week. On our trip, dolphins appeared right in the middle of "I'm Still in Love With You" by Al Green. Most of the week the captain's sound system beeped out celestial, New Age music, during which I have to imagine the dolphins were stampeding toward Bermuda, if only to escape the stereotype. At night we watched a video of musicians plucking out Morse-code guitar into amplifiers underwater—the tune bordered gimpily on the theme from *Deliverance*—and baby-talking into hydrophones: "Hel-lo, dolphin! Do you want to play?" It was a voice that plainly envied the balloon rubbings of real dolphin language, which squeakings, when they arose, had the announcer close to incontinent. "Listen to the excitement! This dolphin defecates from excitement!" (Defecation was a rusty cloud.)

The production ended with a musical dialogue, in which humans had the inferior lines:

HUMAN: I want to be a dolphin! And laugh and play all day!

DOLPHIN: I want to be a human! And find out why they act that way! I'll find out why they fuss and fight! I'll lead them back to the light!

One day, somewhere less than all the way back to the light,

two smooth characters from a hated cruise ship—they'd been spoiling our horizon—came over in a Zodiac to ask if we'd seen any dolphins. "We're from the Cousteau Society," one of them said. I watched in blank apprehension, as though they were on TV; it seemed not to have occurred to me that the question awaited an answer. In fact, nobody answered; we all sat there slack-jawed, parentless, Lori and Lillian and Kay, a pale attorney from Kansas, and Andrea from Hummelstown, sunning with her eyes closed, and Brian contemplating a soda can, and Nancy from Santa Fe holding a sunhat in place with one hand and stretching her toes. Thoughts like "Intruders. I don't like them" and "Are they real?" reverberated a long time in dolphin alpha-wave literalness until finally the captain emerged. "These boats have an agreement not to come within a half mile of each other," he said, glaring. "It's a big ocean."

"Those guys are ruining it here," someone whispered later. "I really noticed a bad energy. I think the dolphins prefer us because we don't chase them."

And yet we did chase them. I'd had my first true dolphin encounter, after all, only when I paused long enough from chasing them that they could follow me to the boat. Which seemed a simple enough dolphin lesson, but humiliating. It meant that your selfish agenda was your own worst enemy, a kind of curse, and you carried it with you everywhere, the ball never leaving your court.

When dolphins answer people's questions, they sometimes overanswer, making you feel stupid for asking. Or they swim right through your question to something more relevant, often food. In 1986 scientists lowered speakers in mid-ocean to see if low-frequency sounds would attract sharks, an experiment that ended when sharks ate the speakers. "They're telling us to stop asking questions and listen," a crew member said. "If you listen, you'll find out how to change the world." ("Change the world" was a phrase she used generically; it covered any creative labor.)

Swimming with dolphins "changed my life," read one letter in the *Project Dolphin Newsletter.* Were our own lives changed yet? We weren't sure. We had tans. In the tanning area of life, we were very changed. Lillian said she was going to study whatever she wanted when she got back to Berkeley and let the uptight business majors hang themselves. I promised Kay from Kansas City that I'd go to the beach more often and maybe even move to Santa Barbara, writing down "Santa Barbara" in my notepad, so the epiphany would survive the trip home.

It was about this time, the fourth day, that we hit upon our "Pod Plan." On the local rumor that dolphins were attracted to creatures who swam communally, in formation, the eight of us were going to organize into a pod, hold hands, and float across the swells, a giant human quilt. And we were all set to try this out when the captain's wife ate a bowl of conch stew and collapsed allergically, and we had to make an emergency crossing back to land, possibly for good.

New Jersey Dave stood over his big canvas bag and leaned on his hands to push down a freshly folded towel. He had on long pants, a polo shirt, and dock shoes, and he was licking his lips. Everyone half-stared at him. He looked like a completely different person on land.

Gail was moving across the dock to the public showers, carrying a hairbrush and a small bath bag. Up to that point we'd been bathing in the sea. Dip, climb out and lather, dip again.

Dave looked up at the sky, then at the captain. "How is the patient?" he said suddenly. It looked like it wasn't what he meant to say originally.

"Well, she's steadier. I think she's probably a little scared. We're going to run her into town, and we won't know much until then."

Dave nodded slowly. He looked at the sky again. "This cab driver you told us about—Mr. Shark? He charges ten dollars a head to Freeport?"

"Sharp—Sharp's Cab."

"Sharp," Dave repeated, tapping his foot. "Mr. Sharp." He did a nervous scat: "Sharp, Shark, Sha-hoooo."

Gail disappeared into the showers.

"I think what Gail and I will do," Dave said, "is get a room in Freeport and look into seeing some of the other islands. Unless . . . I guess there's no way of us finding out if you're going back to the dolphin site tomorrow."

Byrnes said, "You can call the marina here. Leave a message, and we'll let you know if we're going back."

But they never called.

Lori said, "I knew they wouldn't. You could tell."

I asked her if she thought we were going to have any more dolphin encounters.

"Oh, yeah. I know we are." She had a big firefighter's voice, a voice full of hormones.

I asked how she knew, and she said it was something she could tell when we were headed back for land and four dolphins rode the bow to send us off.

That night I fiddled with a portable radio and accidentally found the NBA Radio Network, on which LA was eliminating Portland from the Western Conference Finals. An obscure announcer howled through a blizzard of static. I rooted for the Lakers and then afterward felt blood-gorged, as if I'd eaten meat for the first time in a month. The worldly event felt redundant, a closed system, a culture relevant only to itself.

Maybe it was a culture afraid of losing its job as a culture—afraid of people finding out that the security they worried about was a substitute all along for the real security of living for each other. And everyone should come swim with dolphins and find this out for himself. The Bahamas could then be the new Haight-Ashbury, but much more expensive to fly to.

Lori had guessed right: The captain's wife was doing well and recovering in the care of some neighbors. That meant we would return to the dolphin site, and we might yet have the Ultimate Encounter. Not that I felt shortchanged by my earlier ones. For the next day and a half we had lots more like those: goofy, ecstatic, halftime spectacles where everyone, human and dolphin, swirled around one another, wondering how we all looked, playing this new game. TS was there a lot. Mothers brought calves with white-haloed bellies and bills like ball caps, smooth foreheads demurring in the hypnotic traffic.

But I wasn't sure I'd had any one moment of unmistakable connection, and each encounter ended early—abruptly, it seemed to me. I'd climb out of the water and demand to know what happened to our *Pod Plan.* People plain forgot themselves was what happened. Kay and I would float near the ladder, reaching for other hands that never came. We'd remind each other no violent splashes, and then someone would yell, "Dolphin!" and cannonball off the stern. Lillian sat jackknifed on the bow sprit, holding one knee, swearing she'd be mellow next time. Next time, a pair of dolphins swam right underneath, and she just about pounced on their backs. I tried to make her feel guilty about this, and succeeded, though later everyone's photos proved she was more popular with the dolphins than anybody.

Finally, one day—the last day—an encounter began the same as all the others but ended differently. There were about ten dolphins and a handful of snorkelers in the water. TS was gliding at the fringe.

Suddenly, all the other dolphins just seemed to vanish, extras on the dance floor. We weren't facing each other, TS and I—we were parallel. But the distance between us steadily telescoped, and while I thought warmly how nice it was to see TS one last time, her smile started to open. Like a crocodile's. Slowly at first, then enormously, a monstrous, photogenic laugh, which I returned—I had reached my

Nirvana—and, at that precise instant, the water turned cloudy. "My God," I whispered. "TS has defecated with excitement."

It unfolds that TS was barfing.

Specifically, TS barfed up a squid pen—a special event in itself, at least to Pamela Byrnes, because it suggested strongly that the spotteds do feed in deep waters. And it wasn't TS after all, but someone who reminded me of TS. Anyway, I enjoyed myself.

The spell of the dolphin expedition lasted exactly three days, a period during which the floor of my apartment rolled like waves, and police sirens sounded as if they were many, many doors away.

Summer was about to begin in LA, but for several years, I'd had the encroaching sense that the whole subject of LA summer was graying at the temples—not just in the case of beach-movie LA, but also with regard to those Beachwood Canyon brownstones where Jim Smith had lived, and where no one had seemed, at least during working hours, to work. Awaiting me, if I wanted it, was a date with a conflicted, introverted sexpot in reformed-junkie black jeans who thought I was a real writer; we'd be heading, in a yuppie-foodie-hipster omen, to the first-ever Taste of LA event downtown—people now went downtown. For I'd been pushed east along with many, first to Echo Park, then to Angeleno Heights. And the drive to the ocean, in a city ever more dense, could feel . . . transatlantic. But if you timed it just right—if you wrote in the mornings, packed a lunch, drove to Pacific Palisades and swam, alone with the gulls, as the fog was unbreaking, you would remember why you wrote phrases like "Santa Barbara" in your notepad.

Lillian tried to deny she was back in LA by going swimming in her pool with all her snorkel gear on.

Lori sent me a letter: "Don't procrastinate. The dolphins have things they want to tell the masses, and you are a vehicle." She misspelled Edgeware Road, my street, and it came out "Edgewater."

The day the floor stopped moving, I was conscious of it stopping. I looked at the floor, and it was just like a floor. It was very unhypnotic. The thought that glided by was: *These might be the last seconds of remembering there's nothing in the world to worry about.* And the next thought was: *What did I mean by that?*

3

Pool Man

Every March is free hot dog month at Superior Pool Supply—an early sign of summer, at least to pool men in Norwalk.

"You're about out of relish," John the pool man said, finishing his second.

Someone said, "You know, hot dogs didn't used to come with relish."

The Latinos at the counter smiled at each other without smiling, the way everybody does in trades without women.

Thirty or forty years ago there may actually have been more women in the pool business. But even today the rows of industrial products had barely changed, timeless in white/orange packaging, along with the ancient elements of chlorine cakes and bottles of Solar Blanket. Outside, the parking lot was blazing and still, and it was easy to imagine forward or back to the part of middle-late summer when it's so horror-movie hot that no one can hear you scream.

Then John and I drove back to Seal Beach across prairies studded with oil wells, and the very best thing about driving to other people's pools in the middle of the day might be that you get to feel connected in some semiofficial way to the debut of summer, while not so connected as to live and die by the events of a particular backyard. As anyone who grew up in California knows, there's as much ache as joy around man-made reservoirs ("To my left was an empty swimming pool, and nothing ever looks emptier than an empty swimming pool," wrote Raymond Chandler); for every memory of diving and splashing to exhaustion in my Valley childhood, I've got another one of nursing wounds, numbing out, and all the fatal, carnal pleasure of doing that—simultaneously intoxicated, dazzled, and victimized by water and light. Just the sight of an unused pool in summer still brings up afternoons in socks and shoes on restriction. And I might never get over a July when I was nine, a pissed-off child of a divorce, right arm in a blinding-white cast that I suspended bitterly above the tile coping in order to wade.

Back then there were four archetypes of pool design, like great faiths of the world: Each seemed to have missed, by the narrowest, most tragic margin, the paradise it was meant for. 1) 1950s rectangles, Spartan as biscuits; these belonged to the poorer, happier families in the neighborhood and their surfboarding dogs. 2) Reedy Xanadus, like the pool in *The Twilight Zone* episode where the brokenhearted children swam away to caring families through a warp in the deep end. 3) Turquoise kidney shapes of the 1960s. 4) Cantilevered Greco-Spanish altars. Since the 1970s, though, relatively few pools have been built for the middle class, which is why so many customers today are very old, while the pools themselves exist like gorgeous crypts in a suspended animation of maintenance.

Hence, pool men—who are serfs, obviously, but also independent, unbeholden, Chandleresque. They're ghosts of the jingle-jangle morning, whistling arrival with a wood gate slamming behind them. To my childhood self, their comings and goings looked like the height of Pied Piper free agency. So much so that decades later, blocked and confused, when *The Artist's Way* prescribed making list after list of alternative careers, I'd invariably write down: Pool Man.

As for John, he was a family friend—I was writing about a churchy, slightly geeky pool guy. Although he had fingers as thick as an outfielder's mitt and could probably tear off a frozen gas valve at the stem, he was trim and bespectacled, and his idea of cursing was to gasp: "My word!" He had a sandy red business major's beard trimmed close, and it dropped with his jaw whenever he listened or thought hard on a subject.

Nor was he much of an escapist, but as with a lot of pool men, there'd been a former life (his was in Oil), followed by a moral turning point: He'd sued his uncle and grandfather for defrauding the family business, and won. He did that for his mom, and because the older men in the family didn't believe him when he said that he would.

How John got his pool route was by buying someone else's, for the going rate of six to nine times a month's revenue. To John's mind that was robbery. But the failure rate was low, and if you lost a client, you didn't lose much: $40 to $80 a month, which is both too little to charge and too much to spend. (You can get a xenophobic lecture on immigration and deflated service fees by asking around any pool cleaners' association meeting.) Happily, the learning curve was almost nonexistent—"Any monkey with a cleaning pole can do it," insiders said—although the repair side required training and talent. It took less than three days for John to grasp that he could do pools more efficiently and profitably than the mentor he bought the route from, a onetime attorney who, inaugurating his own quest for invincible summer, had apparently been disbarred for drinking.

John's wife, Barbara, might have had the tougher adjustment to his new job. Everything she thought was great about John in laboratory form—an unpretentious guy, impervious to status, totally attentive to anyone who wanted to converse—had become the dominant gene now, calling her bluff. Once, *Forbes* magazine dismissed a new cologne for the masses with a sentence: "Your pool man can wear it."

Video porn involving pool men constituted a genre all its own. Right off, Barbara worried about housewives in Palos Verdes whom John might see sunbathing. They went back and forth awhile before he told her, "Get over that, and look at who I am."

Lately, she'd been focusing her energies on upgrading his business with professional touches. She recommended coupon books for monthly billing, polo shirts with logos, and magnetic signs for the doors of the truck. To John these were great ideas but almost heatstroke tiring to think about after a long day, as one summer followed another.

What he liked best about having a pool route was that he was outdoors, and that there were repair problems just tricky enough to challenge him but not defeat him. What I liked best about riding with John was seeing summer arrive one day at a time and watching him listen to the customers talk about their lives—like *Highway to Heaven,* a show I'd never actually seen. Plus it reminded me of the consolation I used to feel working in restaurants on New Year's Eve, to be one of the servers instead of the lonelies at the banquet, with all their good-life expectations.

The loneliest of John's lonely customers was an old woman named Mrs. Wadsworth, whom even John had begun to avoid. She had a two-story lanai house with mint-green siding and in her driveway sat an oxidized Ford Tempo with one flat tire. We waited there a few minutes watching a van drive slowly up the street twirling newspapers out of both side windows.

"She's always got a question about her bill," John whispered. "And she's having health problems. You can tell she might have been really pretty once. But she's one of these people who takes a breath in the middle of a sentence, so you can't get a word in to be helpful." Recently she was given to suspicions that someone—maybe a gardener, maybe John?—had stolen her pole skimmer.

On the floor of the pool moved a vacuum pump in the shape of a giant breathing flower. John started trailing his net along the surface, capturing a lot of wet leaves. In a couple of minutes the pool looked happily used, as if it had been swum in. With a net stuffed with chemical test kits and chlorine tabs, John started back toward the gate, but he would not get there. Mrs. Wadsworth had opened the sliding glass door and stood gathering herself to speak with her head lowered as if she were trying first to swallow.

"I don't know who took my net," she said at last. "Who would *do* something like that, John?"

There was no way to answer. In any event, John had brought along a replacement, spending all of ten dollars. "I'm only charging you a thousand," he said, winking. After an apparently conflicted pause, he asked her how she felt today.

She said, "I feel awful. My house is no longer my own, John, and when you've lived as long as I have—*never* did I have a dirty house, and I raised three children here, and they all learned to swim at McGaugh Elementary."

"What year was the pool built?" I asked.

"February nineteen sixty-nine," she said, which meant that Mrs. Wadsworth had been young with the Beatles.

Afterward I asked John if he felt any desire to stop humoring this woman—to break through, take a risk, beg her to stop settling for a victim's consolations—and he seemed to actually brighten up thinking about it. "You might be right. What would I have to lose? I'd almost gain if I lost her as a customer."

We were getting to very few homes. A wicked Santa Ana over the weekend had turned the pools into twiggy marshes. ("For seven years, I hated wind," a former pool man told me, closing that chapter of his life.) The benefit of this was that the day broke amazingly clear, an expectant, fragrant-desert morning. In the older neighborhoods, the blue-trimmed Craftsman houses looked like sailor shirts, and you could hear the chink of a tetherball chain from a nearby schoolyard. But along the route, residents stood outside as if there'd been an accident. "Nothing's working," said a woman in her backyard beside an overwhelmed filter pump.

The other reason John was behind was that he'd spent Monday attending a memorial service—a brutal one, for the week-old baby of a certain young couple. The mother, maybe not surprisingly, was having nobody's formulaic compassion; in fact, her eulogy accused the gatherers of taking life for granted—of not deserving life, of being deader than her baby. "We are the dead ones!" she screamed. Then, at a critical moment, she actually opened the casket in order to pray for a resurrection—as in, why pray for a resurrection if you don't have faith enough to watch it happen?—which gesture had been too much for some people to bear. The baby did not resurrect, but everyone left knowing what kind of loss a memorial was supposed to be about.

We weren't long done with this discussion when we visited Mrs. Stewart, a forty-ish woman with a cigarette in a filter holder who announced that her husband's lung cancer had returned.

John stood with his head tortoised forward and his hands on his hips. "Oh, my word. I am sorry to hear that."

She took an impatient drag on the cigarette, half-turning toward the house; she was not going to go too deeply into this.

"This is a writer," John announced, sensing some confusion. "He's actually writing about me. The Life of a Pool Man."

"You know, when I saw him with you, I thought: Don't you leave me now, John. I thought you were giving your route to someone!" She looked at me. "John's the best there is. I'd give up Poopsie before I gave up John."

The late afternoon was starting to turn cold, which on top of a sunburn felt like missing the last bus of the day. At Bixby Hill in Long Beach, nicknamed "Pill Hill" because a lot of doctors live there, a former actor named Mr. Baggett tried to explain the solar panels up on the roof. Wind was mucking up the water, and you could hear neighbors making their dinner and John's knuckles banging around to get the truck properly loaded.

"Have a good evening," John said, waving once.

"Well," Mr. Baggett said, turning the word toward a Ronald Reagan moment, "having a chat with you fellows is part of *having* a good evening. I thank you for coming!" Then he was hustling indoors, too, as if he realized all at once that this was only March, false summer having fooled everyone into going without jackets.

An aerial view of California today would show more than a million pools in the ground, as many pools as there are residents of Nevada—evidence of an overpowering instinct to either lay down our burdens by water, or never leave the suburbs, or, like Dustin Hoffman in *The Graduate,* be gorgeously dead for a summer. The grandest version of that daydream to date was that of the Anthony Brothers, whose business began in the late 1940s when they dug their own pool by hand out in Hawthorne and the neighbor over the backyard fence asked for one of the same. Nowadays, Anthony & Sylvan has diversified into ski equipment and fishing supplies, and you get the impression that the business has had to do some growing up.

At the service level, fees are pinched to the point of near humiliation. You can make $40,000 or $50,000 a year cleaning pools if you never rest, only to have a customer decide he wants you summers only, when your chemical costs quadruple. John also complains about pool-supply stores that offer cleaning service directly to the public, often underbidding him. At night, pool men grouse about such subjects over the Internet.

They also talk shop about everything from parts per million of dissolved solids to solutions for cracked, winter hands (vitamin E lotion under disposable latex gloves). And they network for things like sick-route coverage and liability insurance: Gone, in our litigious age, are the metal ring-toss games that kids won by seeing who could hold their breath underwater the longest. In the swimming-pool business, fantasies of paradise are often giving way to the realities of accident and aging. Robert Altman's *Short Cuts* depicted a pool man's disillusion at the end of a workday:

a two-income apartment and a wife who sells phone sex.

What doughnut shops are to police, Ecco's Pizza parlors are to local pool cleaners, several of whose associations convene there one night a month. ("Wayne's going to explain the new life-insurance card," announced a United Pool Association secretary, upon which Wayne stood up and said, "Real quick, I don't know if everybody knows this, but you receive one hundred percent coverage for the following: loss of both hands or both feet, loss of entire sight of both eyes, loss of one hand and one foot, loss of one hand and entire sight in one eye, loss of one foot and the entire sight of one eye, loss of speech and hearing in both ears. A hundred percent.") There, I picked up a few tales about dog bites and pratfalls and novice pool men who flooded a home by running a drainage line from a pool to a toilet, or who over-chlorinated the hair off a rich man's shins. John himself once fell into a pool—in winter, off an unhinged diving board that he'd bellied onto to fix a light beneath. There'd been a group of kids watching, and according to Barbara, John went home shook up, and a little upset at himself.

In most pool-man anecdotes, though, the subtext is status: the pool man as itinerant conscience, standing at the fringe of a hedonist wedding. Living in two very divergent realities are Keith Moon—who got drunk and drove a luxury gas guzzler into the pool of a Holiday Inn on his twenty-first birthday—and the pool man who greeted him afterward. "I figured they'd be so grateful I was alive, they'd overlook the Lincoln Continental. But *no,*" Moon told

Rolling Stone. "There's only one person standing there, and 'e's the pool cleaner. And 'e's furious."

You could learn John's routine in a jiffy. Enter a neighborhood, often past a checkpoint or a sign (WINDWARD POINTE, EST. 2000). Dash surfactant from a squeeze bottle across the water, brush tiles like they're oversize molars. Sometimes break down a filter system, which is composed of diatomaceous earth (pool water is purified, all too poetically, by microscopic sea fossils). Mix and shake chemicals in their plastic jiggers to the right pH, a sunrise pink.

Almost all of John's pools were white, with a very occasional clove-gum gray, for the illusion of a shady lagoon. In one backyard, a hand-painted sign with a singing lovebird read: *Come into my garden and dream your cares away.*

Mrs. Wadsworth had a few cares still to dream away. During this week's visit, speaking through her screen door, she took ten minutes explaining in needless detail that she would be sending John her February check early because she wanted the amount reflected on her March statement, did he understand? Halfway satisfied, she reopened the subject of the missing pole skimmer, which John, on a lucky hunch, bent over and found behind a heater shed.

She didn't seem that excited. Anyway, the net had been torn through. "The gardeners must have stuck it back there," John said.

"My husband built that shed," Mrs. Wadsworth remarked with visible pride. "All nuts and bolts. He didn't use a single nail."

We asked how she was doing.

"Ha!" Mrs. Wadsworth blurted, almost rejuvenated. "I think I should just roll over. Do you know why, John? I want to do all the things I'm no longer able to do."

John said, "You should come outside maybe, and enjoy the day."

Mrs. Wadsworth just lowered her head, until it was touching the inside of the screen.

In the presence of a matriarch (in the presence of almost anyone, but especially older women), John comes across as half minister, half inadequate son, solicitous to a level that a more driven pool man—a pool man with a magnetic car sign!—might not be. The thought of disrespecting a customer seemed to offend his sense of chivalry more than mute servitude could. Once, to fix a leak for a housewife in Lakewood, John brought in a certain legendary repair artist—a frogman, someone the United Pool Association members stood in stark awe of—a man who, as it turned out, lost patience with the customer's ignorant hovering. "Would you explain the problem once more to my husband?" she said, handing the frogman her phone. And he replied, "I don't have time to talk to your husband." Instead he passed the phone to John (who ultimately took the fall, getting fired for the whole fiasco), then walked off the job in his wet suit.

That made John indignant. Not the loss of $50 a month, but the principle. And he should never have recommended a contractor he didn't know anything about. Feeling guilty, he spoke out at the next UPA meeting, letting everyone know how the frogman behaved. "Could you imagine doing that to a client?" he said wild-eyed to me. "It would be like telling off your parents. It would be like telling off Mrs. Wadsworth!"

One thing John respected about his own parents was that he always knew where they stood. His father liked arguing so much that he kept an abacus behind his wet bar to keep track of trivial bets, and John himself often doesn't realize that an argument has gone past casual until it's too late. The upside to strong opinions is that he isn't afraid to butt in and sound presumptuous, if he just happens to be standing outside someone's sliding glass door with an answer to their problem. One time, to help resolve a customer's family squabble (two brothers-in-law at war over some work done to the house), John barely hesitated before introducing a game called Conflict Resolution, which resembled hopscotch. (We got out of John's truck and stepped over to the sidewalk; it was demonstration time.) First, he explained, you stand dead center in the first box and state your ISSUE. Then you hop to three lateral declarations, side by side:

I FEEL _____   I WANT _____   I THINK _____

Then you end with two mighty hops forward:

I PROPOSE _____

I'M COMMITTED TO _____.

John landed with both feet and looked up solemnly, still plainly moved by the whole idea of that last sacrificial leap.

He didn't tell me specifically how the parties came to terms. Only that they did, and the family thanked him.

A couple of times I thought: *I'm on the wrong pool route. I've picked the wrong guy.* When I started out riding with John, I was looking for things like: 1) the way summer used to look, 2) a cushy dropout job, 3) an alternate reality, the kind in which my mom and her friends used to work and play in the Valley sun, seemingly free from cares and cancers, 4) I wanted my mom back (who died in winter 1996), plus my dad (winter 1991), and my oldest sister (winter 1999), and 5) not to die the way my mom did, too ashamed to let her wrinkled skin be seen in a bathing suit and obsessed with gadgets breaking down in her house.

I could have picked Steve Schmidt—the same pool guy who told me that he hated the wind nonstop for seven years. A local fine artist, Schmidt brought a genuine dropout's spirit to the job; all he'd ever wanted was "a steady route of pools with good suction." (Windless heat, concrete permanence, the unrent waterline—this was a nirvana I understood.) He considered the poolside aesthetic of light and surfaces to be "meditative" (the sound alone, "all silent but for the motor," could induce a posthypnotic state). And he said he wanted to work that influence into some paintings he was doing at the time.

So for the first few years, he drove around shirtless in the conceptual installation that was the Inland Empire, not only basking in my dream job but rubbing it in. So efficient was Steve's routine that he jumped into each pool after cleaning it, lit a cigarette walking back to his truck, and pulled up dry at the next house in time with his last puff.

True, the long-range picture was terrifying. All the men who stayed in the business long term, Steve said, turned into lizardly mechanics. And he was so bad at repairs that whenever he flicked on a pool light he was surprised if it worked. On the other hand, he could eat mushrooms and sit on somebody's dirty diving board for hours with his Walkman on, just vacuuming the deep end with an extension pole that swore to him it was part of his arm. And he got invited to big, drunken-sheriff parties. "Just bring yourself and a bottle of chlorine," the owners joked.

Once, Steve said, he saw a pretty girl lying naked on top of a patio awning, which may have seemed for a moment a good place not to be watched. He ignored the girl and finished cleaning. But the aunt, who lived next door, caught him smiling. "You look like the cat who ate the canary," she said. He ignored that, too.

Now, what is it, anyway, about exhibitionists and pool men? A woman I knew sunbathed nude every day in a University Estate backyard, visitors coming and going, while her grandfather, the only dad she'd known, lay dying inside the house—her youthful privilege while it lasted, but I used to wonder how their pool man read her message: *Look at me (but don't)? Pretend we're in Eden (but we're not)? Save me from this body of death?* You can practically see the crone within the maiden, all the romantics gazing at their pools from the other end of old age; you can practically hear them ask, "What went wrong?" For thinking there was still enough summer left to be healed by a swim in his pool, Jay Gatsby got shot on a raft, an outcome we have to wonder if he wanted. The convergence of Death Wish with Backyard California is a motif worthy of Melville. "Have you seen the movie *Gods and Monsters?*" Steve Schmidt asked me when we first sat down to talk. More than *Prince of Bel Air* or *Earth Girls Are Easy,* this is the movie that, according to the veteran pool cleaner, came closest to truth. In it, a home-owner tries to provoke his gardener to kill him.

Indeed, one of Steve's own customers, a "frail professor who raised pugs" (the dogs kept falling in the pool, Steve kept saving them), spent a season drinking White Russians in his boxer shorts by the pool and then shot himself, but survived. As soon as he got better, he introduced himself as a cuckolder to the biker next door, who crushed his head with a baseball bat.

"Most of the time," another pool man told me, "it's lonely old women with hair where there shouldn't be hair who want to chase you around the pool." One customer offered him her body in exchange for a false report to a heater-warranty company. Another beckoned him to join her in the hot tub ("Mind if I just sit here and watch you clean?"). This isn't the subject he hoped we would talk about, being a repair enthusiast himself. His goal was to "work till my eyes bleed and make money"—to which end he had cleaned pools in Los Angeles, Apple Valley, Victorville (where the young families with children had gone), Las Vegas (where you could literally jump across most of the pools), La Habra, San Bernardino, and Diamond Bar. He used to drive from Palm Springs to Anaheim and then to Redding in a single day, and he carries in his wallet a photo of his parents, circa 1967, manning their first Anthony's Service Center store.

His ambition had cost him, however. When he transferred to Las Vegas, his own wife and children refused to go, voting family values. He lasted there a year before missing the family and moving back home, and things are better today, but he never finds time to join them in the pool.

For the record, I know a few things about fathers and lost chances, my own dad having swum in our brand-new Anthony pool less than a handful of times before he divorced from my mom in the 1960s—the ground no sooner dug than a disappointment. Except there was this one afternoon when I climbed up his knee, stomach, chest, to be flipped into the shallow end—over and over, as often as I asked, filling a need the size of a pool.

Contrast John, neither the escapist pool man nor the ambitious pool man so much as the pool man on the firing line of life, going from one strange sitting room to the next, offering his vagabond take. One day we got news of an actual death. Having lost her husband, Pete, two years ago—pneumonia had set in after a dental infection—Evelyn Katzaroff, a sixty-two-year-old schoolteacher, had now lost her husband's brother, Al.

In portraits around the house, Pete Katzaroff smiled a big Ed McMahon smile, sometimes over the neck of a guitar. He designed their pool, too, which included a fountain from the mouth of a lion. A son—onetime Florida Marlin

Robbie Katzaroff, whose photos have a room of their own—still holds the UCLA record for career triples.

Mrs. Katzaroff said she figured she'd retire now.

"That might be a good decision," John said. A second later his eyes warmed and he nodded relief, as if he were suddenly seeing a good end to what started off bad. "Maybe, you know, you've been using work in a way just to cope. Now your grandkids will get you."

She agreed with that. "It's just that I always felt Pete was going to make it."

John said, "That dentist should have given antibiotics."

"He's with Al now. I wanted to tell you that," Mrs. Katzaroff said. "Al sat up in his hospital bed, right at the end, with his family around him, and he told his wife, 'I want to go to Pete's mansion! And I want the living waters!'"

The worst section of John's route in Long Beach resembled the Deep South. There were power-line towers, dead lawns, and a cracked plastic Aqua Slide stamped BROWNVILLE, TX. At a public-housing pool, John's net scooped up AA batteries, a Brass Eagle air-gun cartridge, a rock, a coat hanger, a Reebok, a Kit Kat wrapper, several cigarette butts, and numerous plastic train tracks.

The wealthiest section, which was practically next door to the poorest section, had plantation-style balconies, gabled fences, pine trees, London lampposts, a languid beach towel, and bottles of serious suntan lotion. A customer in pleated shorts and spotless tennis shoes with clean stretch socks waved from his garage, chomping a cigar. He was stacking some things, and he had a rich man's way of getting it done, as if some unmarked boxes on the clean garage floor had drawn him into a challenging, but not unpleasant, game of "work."

It was in this neighborhood that we ran into a Nigerian prince. We were driving at a gawker's pace, grabbing real-estate handouts as souvenirs, and a single small car bore down upon us from the other way, as if in a low-speed game of chicken. The driver parked and got out with the key alert chiming. He was a white-haired African in vague ceremonial attire—a black robe with gilded lions, which I managed to ask about.

"Why, I'm from a royal family in Nigeria," he began. "I'm worth"—his tongue tricked out the figures in a sharp cadence—"one hundred and twenty-five million dollars. I'm going to be establishing a ministry around here. I have a crown, too. Would you like to see it?"

"That's all right," I said, as he steered me toward his rented Chevy. "Sure, okay!"

He placed it in my hands, a stiff braided skullcap studded with gems.

"My friend John over there," I remarked confidingly, attempting to impress the prince, "is a very serious Christian."

"That right? You fellows looking for a home, too?"

"I clean some pools around here," John said.

"Oh—well, maybe I'll use you one day!" The prince's

teeth were tusky yellow. And now there was a pause. "Shall we pray?"

So we seemed to be joining hands in the middle of the road, a bristle-bearded pool man and an African prince and me, Krusty the reporter, looking over my shoulder to see who might be watching through parted curtains while dialing the police.

The prayer began with strands of Psalms and Scripture ("Wherever two or more are gathered . . . the wisdom of the Lord is perfect . . . he who dwells in the secret place of the most high . . ."). Then it lifted up into a trembling, pitch-pipe kind of song ("I—love—the Lord—He's—so—good—to—me") that settled back down at last into dry silence on the old man's tongue. Afterward, he got our mailing addresses and gave us both high-fives. "It's all God's money," the prince said.

Only John heard him differently. John distinctly heard him say, "I'm going to buy you guys a home."

"A home . . . each?" I said.

"I don't know! I just heard, 'you guys a home.'"

"I didn't hear that at all," I said.

But I imagined us moving to the neighborhood, separately or together, and swimming in our pools all day and night (while the regular residents disappeared, a sort of Rapture in reverse): Pool Man Heaven.

Through all this, though, John's customers were dying in earnest. After Al Katzaroff, it was Jim Stewart, the husband who couldn't stop smoking. We watched him being helped to the passenger seat of a car headed to Kaiser. "Don't just pray for him to hang around," said his wife. And when he died, she told John, "Don't you leave me now."

The same day, we drove to see Mrs. Wadsworth, who not only hadn't died, but had let me talk her into being interviewed.

"I've got history, baby," she'd told me earlier on the phone. "I'm a survivor. But I'm not surviving now. Listen to me. I'm a doer, a shaker, a rattler, and a roller. I taught my kids to flutter-kick in that pool. I bet you never heard that word either. But for two years I haven't been able to do the things I want to do. I can't get on with my life," she explained, "until these neighbors cut back these trees out of there! And they're both mad at me now, and it's breaking my heart—I've never had a neighbor mad at me!"

My fantasy was that in her living room, Mrs. Wadsworth would warm to the subject of her life after all. But when we got there, she changed her mind about letting us visit. Her daughter had been in a fender-bender—no injuries, but dealing with insurance companies was a nightmare. It would be simply unthinkable for Mrs. Wadsworth to let us see the inside of her house in such disarray. Nor, apparently, could she seem to open the screen door and step outside, not if the house was burning—which, from my point of view and John's, it essentially was. It wasn't hard to imagine that Mrs. Wadsworth would never use her swimming pool again.

Whereas both John and I felt a fair amount of pressure just now to stay young. Having raised four children nearly to adulthood, John and Barbara were assuming custody of two more from an overwhelmed friend. Having managed to keep three kids fed, my wife and I were expecting a fourth child by summer, an unbeatable way to stay young, if you overlooked the fact that you felt finished already. A joyous chance to set the boulder of your life's work back at the base of the mountain, where Sisyphus was young. The truth was, I was depressed and had been ever since I thought up the idea of riding with a pool man. My work was in a drought, and I lacked even the poolside memory of how to revel in shutting down, let alone recapture a child's sense of joy.

That same week, a career coach, a church friend of John's, asked me how things were at home.

"I've been difficult to be around," I said.

He said, "When you have been more successful in your work, have you been nicer to be around?"

"Actually, yes," I said. I felt myself sit forward. "When I'm getting stroked at work, I think I'm much nicer overall."

He looked sad and confident at the same time. "God can't let that attitude continue, Alan." His tone seemed to say we weren't leaving the room until I stopped misdiagnosing my problem.

Then he hugged me and prayed for me (what kind of day would it be if I didn't get prayed over by two guys in an afternoon?), and I drove home thinking the time has come, this could be the day I receive the truth, that my freedom to love and be loved does not depend on how I'm doing in the world. I spent two or three more days sitting around like a yogi, practicing feeling loved, practicing not frowning, feeling like a member of my family, and a success and a child.

The next time I saw John, he was talking to another guy, whom John didn't know, which was funny, because he turned out to be a pool man too. They stood around talking spiritual things, one pool man to another, except the first guy looked strung out and ashen. He said he'd just driven back from Joshua Tree, where he always used to feel all spiritually connected, only this time a voice in his head said, "I'm not here." Which was not the reassurance he'd wanted.

"Oh, my word," John said, his mouth dropping. He went on to explain that of course, if you were seeking Life in an experience of the past, a voice would say, "I'm not here." John's eyebrows were jumping. "Don't you see?"

So let's just say that my time with the pool man was an off-season *Christmas Carol*. The ghost of poolside future is death. And the ghost of poolside past is nothing but a pretty lie.

Whereas the ghost of this summer arrives at a twelve-year-old's birthday party in Mission Viejo in the middle of May. The pool is a brand-new tank above the ground. The chemicals are balanced. The living waters are icy, freaking out the children. I have a stupid knee brace from an old injury, and thinning hair, and my trunks fit too tightly around my wintry stomach, but I can't afford more worry. Both the baby on the way and the baby in the casket say that this is my time. And I plunge in. (Thank you, Mr. Pool Man.) I will never be younger.

4

The Metaphysics
of Hang Time

The subject was hang time: The mystery of jumping into the air, and then staying in the air, heels measurably above the hardcourt, now negligibly above the hardcourt, but above the hardcourt all the same, until they weren't anymore, until they were resting blatantly on the hardcourt, fooling no one. Of necessity, our discussion would be scientific.

"See now," said Elgin Baylor, Hall-of-Famer, Los Angeles Lakers legend. "One person doesn't stay in the air longer than any other. One person might jump higher. And the person that jumps higher will come down after the person that doesn't jump as high. But also what happens is the defensive person, they're the ones that commit themselves first. So they're going to go up first—they're going to come down first. And if you watch, that's exactly what happens."

Baylor was my childhood hero, maybe my first image of a savior, because at a Lakers game when I was five or six, my father informed me he was the player to watch soaring through the paint, the figure on whose shoulders, it was clear, our hopes of victory and justice rode. Yet the same awakening of psychological transference gave birth to knowledge, to worry—an almost inappropriate peek into human frailty. Some of those swooping shots clanked off the rim—maybe half, to be honest—and, year after year, he crumbled in the finals against the Boston Celtics. I'd seen Baylor's secret, I felt, but it made me love him all the more. In high school, I got to attend his weeklong youth basketball camp at the University of Redlands. I'd damaged a retina, of all things, just days before—there's no other way to classify it: a sun-tanning injury—but it was being treated with steroids and special precautions. So it was still conceivable, talking to Baylor all these years later, that he might remember the young camper who'd walked into the gym wearing sunglasses with one lens swaddled in gauze. I decided I probably shouldn't bring that up.

The physicists, I told Baylor, say that if two objects are dropped from a great height above the Earth, one after the other, the distance between them lengthens as they fall because the lower object is nearer to the Earth's center and accelerates always faster than the object above it.

"That's right," Elgin Baylor said.

Believing Is Seeing. Before a basketball player can hang in the air, he has to think to try it—the question, from our modern frame of reference, being why the obvious idea wasn't obvious always. I like coach Jim Valvano's theory. He offered it to *Sports Illustrated* in 1984, only partly tongue-in-cheek, and it centered on the observation that coaches throughout history valued "control"—which, to a vintage coach with cigar in his mouth, meant two-handed set shots with eyes narrowed. In the rickety-gym era, you simply didn't leap before you thought, any more than you shot free throws with your elbow pointing at the scorer's desk, because every cultural verity you knew called it "jungle ball." In 1955, Kobe Bryant and Michael Jordan would have been benched for their imaginations.

Whereas by the twenty-first century they were deified, a measure of how much the game had changed, and almost entirely for the better. Forget about the neoconnoisseur's dissent, which likes to imply that old-school, Celtic-style teams—i.e., flatfooted teams—held a monopoly on teamwork and court sense; it's a racist argument anyway and only feeds the power of what it tries to suppress. For played above the net, basketball elevates itself to a form of saving myth—offers instants of triumph unavailable not only to the average life, but to the average sport. This is a telling point. Precisely because they allow no such Scoring as Statement, baseball and football fields everywhere are trampled by extraneous ritual: a tented-arm reception at home plate, a lineman's sack dance. But the one major sport a kid can practice alone on a playground supplies an imagery to match any gloom he's yet encountered; then it leaves the rim shaking, so he'll remember.

Playing above the net, of course, is not the same thing as *staying* above the net—which is what gives the notion of hang time its mystique. And anyone who doubts the depth of fan willingness to embrace a mystique ought to survey the stands next all-star weekend. I remember a night at the Los Angeles Sports Arena, where real people once could afford seats. Julius Erving took a long step from the foul line and faked rightward with the ball, then raised it high above the defense, torch-bearing through the key, then turned it over in the air and cupped it low as a lawn bowler when other arms shot up to stop him; and all at once I was aware of an insurgence in the arena, a sort of silent gathering shout, so that when Dr. J pitched the ball underhand into the basket off the glass, not even a real Dr. J move by any standard, more suggestion than actual flight, like a song remembered half-aloud, I looked around the colonnade and saw a peculiar thing: a couple dozen civilians landing, feet first, in the aisles. I mean, I never saw them jump—just *landing,* as if from branches, hurling two-fingered referee's signals at the floor: *Count it!* Then they climbed back politely to their seats. The sporting equivalent of air guitar.

How long Erving was in the air I couldn't say. That he was an aging legend when this demonstration took place is revealing, though, because in a way his mystique did the work for him. A hand-fake, a gesture, the old warrior's bluff that he's holding something back—this stare-down mysticism is unique to a handful of heroic figures, without whom the notion of "hang time" would have been dismissed long ago as the sliver on a stopwatch that it was.

Baylor, who just plain invented the phenomenon, had such carriage eyeing the basket that his opponents looked like ciphers in a spiritual test; Erving offered an updated parallel, the aplomb of an urban sorcerer. Michael Jordan was the 1990s savior, strong-armed and sleek, with the first oversized boxers, shaved head, tongue wagging as loose as a coyote's. Most important, each of these men was a born protagonist. Not even a rival fan could escape the mood of tragic theater in the NBA Finals when Jordan was effectively barred from the lane by a belligerent Detroit defense; he was Superman succumbing to Kryptonite. Nor could that memory outlast his flights of transcendence. In Game Five, when heavy-footed nemesis Bill Laimbeer barreled in to smother a breakaway, Jordan neatly ducked him, slipped a virtual flying headlock, twisted 180 degrees, and laid the ball up backward over his head while the bad guy tumbled off court. Would "hang time" merit attention without the heroic storyline? Was Jordan really in the air longer than Laimbeer? Did he "hang" there longer than physics are supposed to allow? And does it matter?

In other words: Who, but a complete fool, would attempt to parse a miracle?

I Attempt to Break This Down. If Bill Laimbeer were dropped from a height above the Earth, he would fall always faster than a body above him.

Actually, I'm wrong about that, according to a layman's guide called *The Relativity Explosion* by Martin Gardner: Laimbeer would fall faster so long as the play occurred in an elevator rocketing into space (if you like elevators in space, incidentally, and diagrams of men shouting "Hello" from speeding trains, this is your book), because, in such a gravitational field, all objects fall along parallel lines. Take away the elevator, and the paths more likely *merge* on account of the curvature of the Earth. This is a factor Baylor and I managed to omit in our discussion. I am kicking myself, and I assume he is, too.

Now came Steven Frautschi (actually, I phoned him), Caltech Professor of Theoretical Physics, to assert that, even under ideal conditions, Laimbeer's superiority in drop speed would be negligible—though the height of the jump, here, is going to be crucial (a point on which Frautschi and Baylor seem to be of one mind). "The motion your center of mass goes through in jumping," Frautschi said, "is called a parabola. Which is—well, it's a curve, really. Now, what determines how long the center of mass stays in the air is just the speed of takeoff. You're going to have a certain 'speed,' at which you 'launch' yourself." (Frautschi tried to help certain key words along with his inflection.) "Meanwhile gravity's pulling you back down. And that takes a certain amount of 'time.' And the only thing you did that affects that is the speed of your takeoff. Now, these great basketball jumpers; they're good, I suspect, even from a standing jump, because they're, quote, good jumpers. Plus, well, they're artists, which means they can do more with their hands, and that's—that's skill."

We chuckled philosophically.

"But compared to someone who took off just as fast, with the same amount of push in the legs? They aren't in the air any longer at all."

Baylor's point exactly: "Because most of the time, when you're going to the basket, you're going on an angle. But the guy defending against you, he's going straight up, and so usually the defensive man—he's gonna just come down sooner." There was simply no other way to say it. "He's gonna come down sooner! I mean, if you're going on an angle, most of the time, you're going on an angle, so it's like a broad jump, and he's trying to go straight up—he's gonna come down before you are!"

"And inertia?" I asked Frautschi. "What of inertia?"

"Well, if the mass is greater, it's harder to change the motion." Frautschi paused, then adopted a more confidential tone. "In plain English," he said, "it's hard for the real heavy guy to jump as high as somebody of, let's say, equivalent height who's more lightweight. So your best jumpers, in general, are not going to be real heavyweights."

I thought about this.

He clarified: "Because the heavyweight has to exert more force to get himself into the air."

I admitted to Frautschi that sounded logical.

He added, somewhat mysteriously, "It's harder to push a heavy guy around—that's a separate issue."

"Separate, you mean, from heaving himself into the air," I said. "This issue of pushing him someplace."

"Yes. Yes."

A Writer Is as Authoritative as His Sources. So I asked Elgin Baylor about the future of physics.

"I don't think anyone will ever prove there's any secret to

hang time. Because, I'll tell you what. You put Michael Jordan under the basket, and have someone else drive in on him; Michael will come down before them. You never see a defensive man hang in the air. Because if that was the case—they would be sensational! They would block every shot! I mean, they would just hang up there, waiting for somebody to shoot!"

I asked Professor Frautschi to pick the legends of hang time.

"That sixties player you mentioned before. The Laker. Baylor, was it? He was beautiful."

5

The Metaphysics
of Painting

My friend Janet had never seen the Sepulveda Dam. I found this amazing, incomprehensible, possibly untrue; Janet stood by her story. I had to remember that the dam was not part of her childhood. She grew up in San Diego, and Virginia, and Taiwan, almost every place but the San Fernando Valley. (I grew up in the San Fernando Valley—small world.) Though she'd lived in LA, the Wilshire area, for fifteen years as a magazine editor, she postponed learning to drive for the first ten, and thus saw the city almost exclusively through the scored side windows of the Rapid Transit District bus. When finally she climbed into a car of her own, she bounced around in the seat and tooted the horn and practiced the foot pedals and adjusted the rearview, and froze right there in the driveway, and went inside to write a nice essay about the range of new concerns this new freedom had thrust upon her. "Can I take myself anywhere," she wrote in paragraph 10, "or will I dance on tables?" Making it to the dam would take her a while.

Whereas I could never escape it. Joan Didion was always seeing Hoover Dam in her inner eye (ever since she'd had that "explicit" experience of touching her hand to a turbine); I saw my dam from the freeway—from the Haskell off-ramp, to be exact, which afforded the most sudden, astonishing view of the dam and the Valley at once, each in the thrall of the other. Circling the off-ramp, your eye could pursue the elements: the gray concrete, the fields following fields reconfiguring behind the wide wickets of the dam, until, as you rounded the bend, the dam would show you its best face of all—its streamlined omniscience, as it deftly clasped our time and place.

Above, the guardrails and lampposts gave the dam a breath of rendezvous, the mood of a border checkpoint from the past. To a Parisian, of course, or even a local grownup, a 1941 edifice may not exactly have screamed Sacred Icon. But it was my earliest emblem for the Valley, and so kept registering as an archetype, something with the force and flow of prememory. Specifically, and unlike Didion, I wasn't thinking about the power of water. No vaulting concrete girdles, no canyon feats. The Sepulveda Dam was designed to let floodwaters from the Los Angeles River toss and rise in its catacombs underground while the rest of us ran for the hills; when the chambers reached capacity, spill gates would open, unleashing a ten-foot wave upon the cornfields . . . in theory. For about fifty years, the limit had never been reached.

The place had usually been parched, in fact, and popping with dry weeds, and in this respect, it was the perfect dam for the Los Angeles River: a sort of abstract dam, a dam-in-principle, the Emperor's new dam; all its power, its promise of onslaught, was implicit. We were supposed to stare at its stony face and guess.

That, in retrospect, is what I'd done. Even as a toddler, I knew by heart the enlightened look of the dam, its gaze, its grin. Cheshire Dam. This was long before I had any clue what a dam was, or what this one was for. For all I knew it was art.

Which brings me to the painter Edward Biberman. I would not have placed his name before learning of him belatedly as the man who painted "that picture" of the dam. Other people seemed to know all about a trio of palm trees he captured against the bleached face of the Carnation Building on Wilshire Boulevard. He died in 1986.

In the snapshot I saw, Biberman resembled Duke Ellington, whom he had never painted. He did paint Lena Horne, and Aldous Huxley, and Paul Robeson, each in the Hollywood Hills that seduced them from points much farther east. He did the mural for the Federal Building downtown (a 1939 celebration of multiracialism called *Each of Us*), and most of his works were social realistic: tall gestures and tools and torsos stretching T-shirts, workmen arm in arm. It was not such a leap from these dimensions of progress and effort to the forms of engineering he started painting after World War II: freeways, for example, and one familiar dam—a reproduction of which I found in his perfectly titled collection *Time and Circumstance.* "I turned to aspects of man's creativity," Biberman wrote in the accompanying text, "which now had new significance for me after so many years of war's waste and destruction."

So I was looking at this reproduction in the library one Thursday in winter, and my first thought was that this was phenomenal: Biberman had evoked exactly what was symbolic and essential about the dam to *me,* even the high cumulous clouds, the exaggerated, peacetime American skies. *How did Biberman know?* was my question to myself.

But my next thought was that those qualities weren't in the canvas at all; they were in the dam. A Polaroid would serve just as well—unless (a *next* next thought) the qualities were neither in the dam nor on Biberman's canvas but in the filter of my own distorted childhood. Which meant that in all likelihood I would never know what the dam looked like stripped of nostalgia, to a disinterested observer, a stranger to the Valley, if such a person existed and could be talked into visiting a dam on a Thursday afternoon in a downpour.

"Which window should I be looking out of?" Janet asked me, as we sluiced through the Cahuenga Pass onto 101 westbound in my unkempt Datsun. "The right," I told her. "The whole Valley is to the right."

And then we kept quiet for a while, past Woodman and Van Nuys and the 405 Interchange. As regularly as I'd seen the dam from this freeway, it had usually been from the corner of my eye; I'd never *searched* for the dam, and now I was finding it hard to remember exactly where the first look would be available. Pretty soon, though, I saw a little grayish something through the trees. "These trees are taller than usual," I said. Suddenly we were out of the trees, no trees at all. "This dam is smaller than usual," I said.

An understatement. We were virtually on top of the dam now, and it looked like you could hold it in your hand—the Matchbox toy of dams. Janet meanwhile wore a look of distress, glancing first at the dam and then at me; she had not spoken for probably two or three minutes and now she blurted her reaction, "It's . . . TINY!"—as we coasted, stunned, to the base of the Haskell offramp.

From there we drove over to Burbank Boulevard and rolled up onto the service road to park atop the dam, something I'd never done. We walked along the parapet, two umbrellas in the gray rain. And the modern contours were beautiful—Janet thought so, too—but vulnerable-seeming up close, which made me feel sorry somehow. I wanted the dam to have one more chance to perform its optical trick from the freeway, see the periphery glorify the dam, see the era enlarge it—because it isn't possible for anyone but an artist to find the soul of a dam up close, in its gray, cuspid, concrete supports. I mean that I can't say how Biberman did it.

6

Measure the Universe

STANLEY: My aunt used to bring me here as a boy. The roof opens up and the universe is menacing.

SOPHIE: You find that menacing? I say it looks pretty romantic. What's menacing?

STANLEY: Well, the *size.* [pause] Of course, I was smaller then.

—*Magic in the Moonlight,* screenplay by Woody Allen

A mountaintop in Chile, with five giant ivory domes gazing upward. We'd spent a few hours in a control room fiddling with computer images of stars—focusing the telescope by remote. Now the astronomer was performing what seemed like an ironic ritual. He was going outside to have a look at the sky.

So we opened a door and practically fell out of the building into Eternity. The night was clear, and the mountain was so dark I couldn't find my own toes—couldn't see anything but the ancient moon and however many zillions of constant stars. "There's the Milky Way," Mark Phillips said at some point, just to say anything. The view from Earth runs flat across the disc of the galaxy, so a hundred billion layered suns converge into a band of light that pours from one horizon to the other. That's how the Milky Way works.

The great thing about astronomy is that it dignifies all your childlike questions. What's going on out there? If space has a limit, what then? These are first-rate astronomical questions—astronomers mean to answer these questions. How old is time? How will it end? This concerned people like Phillips. Phillips studied supernovas, unthinkably violent exploding stars whose degree of brightness correlates to how close they are or aren't. By establishing the locations of distant galaxies, they could be used as surveyor's marks to the edge of the physical universe—might, in other words, finally enable scientists to comprehend the size of all that is.

In the 1920s, Edwin Hubble grasped that the galaxies were flying apart uniformly in every direction; what eluded people ever since was this expansion's rate, which, played backward like a newsreel to the Big Bang, would settle questions about the universe's size and age. (The size of an expanding universe gives away its age, and vice versa.) The first so-called Hubble constant was crude: objects three and a quarter million light-years away were receding at a rate of 520 kilometers per second—a figure that, on rewind, unhappily found the universe to be younger than the earth.

But a half-century's refinements had brought the matter into meaningful debate.

Here things got truly apocalyptic. Measure such cosmic distances, Einstein promised, whether with supernovas or anything else that worked, and you'd also detect the degree of the universe's curvature in the fourth dimension of Time—a fairly impossible concept for laypeople to grasp, but gravity, science says, is the three-dimensional manifestation of this curve. And to know how much gravity there is in the universe is to see, in every sense, the future crashing in through the now.

Too little gravity, and the universe will expand inexorably. Space-time proves flat and endless; the stars fizzle and die. Too much gravity, and the universe will ultimately implode—space-time swallows its tail. The first case implies that existence had a Beginning, a Big Bang, a God (all this expansion had to start somewhere); the second implies that it was all for naught. Many calculations, coincidentally or not, have pointed toward perfect stalemate—all the cosmic music suspended, en pointe, between two catastrophes.

But one last scenario holds that the universe could collapse and re-explode, ad infinitum, a cycle embedded in Eternity. This idea has its romance, its elegance, its Zen. Hubble's own protégé, Allan Sandage of Carnegie Observatories, a volatile figure with a Nixon-style enemies list, insisted it was proven. This made Phillips and his teammates the sticklers, or maybe the postmodernists: pointing up flaws in measurements; waiting for the truth to seem more obvious. Flirting with inexplicability, chaos, and mess.

"So far," Phillips said, "we're focusing on this issue of whether all supernovas are the same intrinsic brightness." There was special reason to think they were, having to do with the critical mass required for such stars to explode. But the data suggested they were a little complicated—that some fade out faster than others. By scouring the sky night after night, the team had found fifty supernovas in three years (pre-search, it was two or three a year), and they'd chosen twenty-six as useful ones to study. As of the night I was visiting, they'd finished their analysis of half. They smelled the finish line.

I was in Chile to see what a typical night's labor was like, and because every astronomer in the world seemed to be there. The Atacama Desert had the second driest skies on earth (Antarctica was number one). Also, key parts of the heavens were visible only from Southern sightlines. There were twenty-five major telescopes in the Chilean Andes—if Martians flew over Chile, they would probably wave. On nearby mountaintops, all the grails of astrophysics were being sought—such as understanding the Great Attractor (an unseen force pulling the galaxies toward it with the gravity of 20,000 trillion suns). Such as, understanding dark matter (invisible matter that made up something like 90 percent of the mass of the universe). *The New York Times* had described the level of competition in Chile as a "second space race." (In a development worthy of Monty Python, U.S. dominance was challenged at one point by a colossal European project named the "Very Large Telescope.") Recently, aging hippies had informed Phillips that the

Earth's "magnetic center" had shifted, abruptly, from the Himalayas to Santiago, Chile. "Hence," the story went, "all these astronomers."

The assistant director of the U.S.-run Cerro Tololo Observatory, Phillips was gangly and bearded and had a casual way of talking, as though he were chewing on a toothpick. His teammate in the control room, Nick Suntzeff, was balding and mustached and reminded me of Rip Torn. He was writing down the night's menu for the telescope, which worked like a jukebox: slew to the chosen quadrant of outer space—hear the ghastly canistered sound of the 100-ton dome revolving—then dive to the chosen cosmic depth. There were 600,000 square degrees of sky, and 100,000 galaxies in each degree. The task was to photograph as many research priorities as possible before sunrise. A Night in the Life of the Universe.

There was added excitement tonight on two accounts. Following a recent supernova sighting, the incoming e-mails were stacking up. *What's your predix for maximum brightness? What would Sandage's be?*

Phillips sturdied himself to the challenge, crunched some figures, typed out his reply: *maximum brightness is 7 days away.*

The European Southern Observatory at La Silla, 100 miles north, was predicting four days, but Phillips liked his guess. "Would you say, Nick," he prompted his partner, "that our record has been better for the most part than the ESO's?"

Suntzeff's response was a mock-serene "Of course."

The other exciting e-mail arrived from San Francisco around 9 p.m. like a rock through a window. The whole crew stood around in sneakers and roomy Levis and sweatshirts to read. *Space Tether May Be Visible At Dawn!* At first, Phillips was properly cynical. "See what it's like to be an astronomer?"

Hello M Phillips! We have reason to believe the SEDS-2 space tether may be visible over Chile at dawn tomorrow morning. The tether is a 20 km long polyethylene string 0.8 m in diameter hanging from the second stage of a delta rocket . . . Surprisingly it is quite visible given the right lighting conditions . . . extremely interested in your observations . . . If nothing else, it's quite a spectacular sight . . . up to three full moon diameters . . .
—Mike Fennel, Tether Applications

"Mike—up—yours," Phillips said, while composing his real reply, which was a request for more details. But the night had taken an unpredictable turn (a string reflects enough light to look like a comet from earth?—cool!), and the universe felt wayward, space debris falling where it would.

Over several hours Phillips had been working with a fidgety momentum, tapping his pencil to a series of sixties CDs. *The Kink Kronikles. 20 Years of Jethro Tull.* The music added a dorm-room air to what looked like the inside of a submarine. There was track lighting with bare bulbs and transom windows to no place, and Godzilla-movie instrument panels with masking tape to mark the settings.

REAL-TIME DISPLAY. ARCON DATA ACQUISITION. TWO DIMENSIONAL PHOTON COUNTER. CHARGED COUPLED DEVICE. The last one was a video-cam display with 4 billion pixels. The most unromantic of all traditions in astronomy is that constellations are displayed as black spots on a white field—ink splotches, melanoma—because in the days before computer monitors, astronomers got used to looking at photographic plates, which are negatives. A keystroke could reverse the black stars to white, but practically no one ever bothers.

The telescope itself—about the size of a helicopter, perched under the visor of the dome—was a stop on a tour, baroque hardware: Leonardo meets NASA. Astronomers visited it mainly to fix a mechanical problem. To get to it, you could take an elevator, but that meant carrying a carful of warm air up the shaft, which was bad. In the twenty-year life of this observatory, as fainter, farther stars had been studied, image-quality concerns had so intensified that a little unwanted warmth could ruin everything. "If they had to build the big dome again," Phillips said, "they wouldn't," because big buildings invite offices, which attract people, who breathe out vapor. In its obsession with cold, Cerro Tololo had moved all its machinery downstairs and would eventually remove the offices entirely. The building is more valuable as a sheath for the telescope.

Inside the dome everything echoed, and there were steel maintenance rungs up the walls, maybe five stories high. Once, on a visit, Chile's minister of the economy asked if he could climb up. For safety's sake, Phillips tried undiplomatically to deny him. He felt an urgent horrified kick from an aide and overruled himself, and the minister scaled to the top of the tank. Throughout history, a macho ethic in astronomy—loosely, don't complain about climbing step-ladders in the dark—has combined elements of slapstick and horror. Mark Aaronson, at Kitt Peak in Arizona, was one of the 1980s' brightest astronomers, and a creature of quick motions. He flung open a door to look at the sky at precisely the wrong instant: the dome was revolving, and it crushed him fatally between door and jamb. Sometimes, on instinct, a tired astronomer tried to balance a moving tele-scope by holding on to it with his arms, and it swept him up grandly into the sky. He hung and screamed with no one around, finally choosing to drop, breaking a leg or maybe two.

Rough, but not so rough you can't hear astronomy's giants laughing at these new guys with their keyboards. In the old days, astronomy meant straining over eyepieces, sliding hand paddles for focus, teardrops freezing to lenses in the drafty domes. Hubble's pupil Allan Sandage—the aging warrior in the fate-of-the-universe debate—had his roots in that era. In the Southern California that still existed when my parents arrived in the 1950s (back when the scientists were as outsized as the Utopians, who were as eccentric and horny as the evangelists), Sandage was the prodigy in a bomber jacket, widely considered the greatest astronomer of the century. Now, it seemed, he'd become a curiosity. "He would always talk about the Mount Wil-son dining room," Suntzeff said, "which was called the

Monastery, because it was all men, and in the old days they always had to wear ties. So a few years ago, when I was observing and I heard Sandage would be there, a friend and I arranged to walk into the dining room wearing coats and ties."

Sandage "appreciated the joke," Suntzeff said, but in a voice so gentle you suspect it was a complex moment.

In Dennis Overbye's *Lonely Hearts of the Cosmos,* Sandage comes off as both brilliant and sentimental, and distracted by an inability to choose his battles. For nearly fifty years he had worked to rescue Hubble's soul from limbo, bringing that unruly expansion constant—that is, the measure of the rate of expansion—down from 520 to near 50 km per second, implying a universe 20 billion years old, with just enough gravity to collapse and be reborn in cycles—i.e., to oscillate forever. "The twenty-billion-year heartbeat," it's been called. A religious child, Sandage grew up to call the universe a miracle. But corrections by people much younger kept pushing the Hubble number higher, and the universe back into chaos.

Phillips and Suntzeff tended to keep this generational conflict tactful, at times practically offering to split the difference. "The difference between a fifty and a seventy-five," Suntzeff said—and then he laughed. "I mean, if astronomy gets something accurate to better than a factor of two, it's a tremendous achievement."

Phillips pointed to records of two supernovas whose rate of fade suggested a Hubble constant of around seventy, vindicating absolutely no one. "Seventy is like kissing your sister," he said. "It's neither sixty nor eighty. But it wouldn't surprise me if that's what the answer is."

A year earlier, Sandage himself passed through Cerro Tololo, and Phillips questioned how precise the data could have been on a supernova from one of those freezing, teary nights in 1937. There had been, as Phillips saw it, certain inexactnesses with photometry back then. Based partly on a reexamination of the 1937 plates, a newer Harvard study now said the universe was between 9 and 14 billion years old, the youngest and weirdest universe yet.

Sandage meanwhile had been recomputing the Hubble constant by measuring galaxies from the Hubble Space Telescope—rolling the dice and hitting fifty every time.

Tethers can be used to throw objects from one orbit to another. Electronically conductive tethers can be useful to plasma physics experiments.
　　　　　　　　—Mike Fennel, Tether Applications

Please send me e-mail asap to establish that we have a connection.
　　　　　　　　—Mike Fennel, Tether Applications

Grabbing this chance to witness polyethylene-string history, Phillips sent his confirmation. Mike Fennel responded with projected viewing parameters about ten seconds later.

At 4 a.m., Suntzeff was watching the universe slide by, plucking out samples. "Here's 1992BK," he said, pointing to a speck. (Supernovas take many years to fade out completely.) "The supernova went off in the middle of this galaxy, so I'm setting up now to subtract the galaxy's brightness." He took a sip of tea, tearing through a manual for the right lens filter. "The night is clear, so we'll use the opportunity to calibrate a lot of images. But the 'seeing' isn't good" (that is, there were distortions, shimmers caused by the wind) "so we're not going to look so deep." (*Worst seeing I've seen in a long time* is a construction peculiar to astronomy.)

Phillips stroked his beard, scrolling through more weirdly technical e-mails about the distance to the latest supernova. (Astronomers share data pretty freely, unless a couple of teams are in a race to publish something.) "Given 1' seeing and Tonry's distance, plus a good 2048 CCD, we could solve it in three hours, maybe less," e-mailed George Jacoby of Kitt Peak. "There really isn't any hurry—the galaxy isn't going anywhere."

Phillips pointed at the screen. "John Tonry has this idea about 'mottling,' where the more distant the star, the less its light is mottled, so you use that correlation to approximate the distance." The technique gave a Hubble value of about eighty, which would put this particular supernova in a galaxy 13.7 megaparsecs away.

Far away, I had to keep remembering, was long ago. The light from our sun is eight minutes old when it reaches Earth. The explosion we were witnessing now was 40 million years old when we saw it go off. Which put it all of maybe one 500th of the way across the universe—or a

250th, depending on whose Hubble constant you used. In one 20,000th of that time, at its seismic creep rate along the North American Plate, the Los Angeles basin will have already dived off the coast of Alaska. It is weird to think of Earth as practically eternal, yet never quite. You kneel on a trapdoor, praying to a mortal sky. I'm pretty interested in this Great Attractor, personally.

Time to check in on Supernova 1987A, a local favorite. It was the first supernova clearly visible to the naked eye since 1604—i.e., since four years before the invention of the telescope. It made the cover of *Time*. "You can't see it very sharply anymore," said Suntzeff, but the light from the first explosion still "echoes" in the gases of the galaxy, and it will continue to echo for 100 years. In first bloom, the event was so bright that observers wished it were a little farther away. They fashioned masks to shade the lens, converting the 4-meter telescope to the equivalent of a 4-incher, something from a hobby shop.

The discovery was something of a feat. At a neighboring facility, observer Ian Shelton was tracking Halley's comet through a region of the Large Magellanic Cloud, our nearest neighboring galaxy, an opaque sea of dots to you and me, but to Shelton every dot had its place, and the plates looked wrong. He had the prank victim's intuition that one fleck didn't belong. It was bright enough that he wouldn't have likely missed it in the past—bright enough, in fact, to see without a telescope. He worried for a minute about a lot of ways of cross-checking the plates and reshooting the plates before it hit him to look over his head. He did, and became the first person since Johannes Kepler to see a supernova without the use of an eyepiece.

Phillips's and Suntzeff's shares of glory came later. They kept adding details through the years about the supernova, extrapolating backward to the star's history, a form of stellar autopsy. "I think my strength," Phillips said, "is playing with data and seeing things in data, particularly in spectra, that other people don't. I'm not a very good physicist."

Phillips and Suntzeff considered themselves workhorses, long shots in a field littered with failed geniuses—a self-image that in some ways folded neatly into the castaway adventure they were on. Among the Chilean staff, Phillips had been nicknamed "Gilligan," apparently on account of his looks but maybe through deeper associations, too. Liaison to visiting gringos is a role he relishes. He kept warning me, with the trailblazer's secret pride, about maniacal drivers on Santiago's International Highway.

He spent his college years at UC Santa Cruz, next to Watsonville, where the signs say ARTICHOKE CAPITAL OF THE WORLD, a terrain so similar to Chile's that he felt cheated when he got here. "My first night here, one of the scientists' wives said, 'I'm going to serve you a local delicacy,' and she put an artichoke in front of me."

Suntzeff went to Redwood High near San Francisco, circa 1970, in the scientific era of moonwalks and planetary probes. A classmate, he later realized, was Robin Williams: soccer player, nerd. Suntzeff won prizes in math, but in graduate school at Stanford, he came to the cold self-assessment that he might be ordinary. The Mozarts of math were few. Astronomy and physics, on the other hand, could be the stuff of Found Poetry: You only needed to get out there and fact-gather, give luck something to work with.

Once you'd made the cut as an astronomer in the United States (reportedly 100 graduates annually competed for twenty jobs), you could do worse than move to Chile. Suntzeff lived in "The Compound," a hillside colony of a dozen houses adjacent to the observatory's office headquarters in La Serena, a coastal town about the size of Santa Barbara. The homes were prebuilt elsewhere, and the lots were braceleted by rocks like the graves of pets, but they had nice redwood terraces and a view of the Pacific two miles below. Everyone walked to the office in the morning downhill the way water would flow from a runny sprinkler. At 10 a.m., the scientists met for tea in the reading room. At noon, they went home for lunch. A U.S. astronomer's salary in Chile supported a house and family and a housekeeper too, and a seductive retro culture had developed. Visiting astronomers were chauffeured to day rooms attended by cooks and maids. The secretaries dispensed marriage-manual wisdom. When Phillips was new to La Serena, a secretary prevented him from sampling the packets of Boldo tea on display by the coffeemaker. He asked why. She stiffened one forefinger, and then drooped it forward, shaking her head.

Fully thirty-two of the U.S. astronomers in the colony, Phillips included, had married Chilenas. (Suntzeff's wife was Croatian.) Phillips, whose salary as assistant director of the observatory placed him, according to one staffer, "several omegas above the rest of us," lived off the compound in a house worthy of a Hollywood producer. He drove home listening to Jethro Tull and Cream, past low-rent suburbs, past fields of mango, past train cars heaped with iron ore that would return across the ocean as Japanese cars. His wife, Sylvana, was literary and bejeweled, and she let the stars have their mystery. The two never talked about astronomy. Their sons boogie-boarded during the Chilean summer. It was like a U.S. suburb, the 1950s in exile, with science as protectorate.

On a typical list of supernova facts, every item reads like a misprint. In half a second, the density of a supernova multiplies itself by a factor of a million. A core the size of Earth collapses supersonically to the size of Manhattan.

Then it rebounds.

Just the first second's rush of escaping neutrinos—subnuclear flecks that pass through our bodies unseen—carries an energy, Phillips happily pointed out, "surpassing that of all the optic light emitted per second in the entire universe." What Earth's sun will radiate in its lifetime of 10 billion years, a supernova exceeds a hundred times in the blink of an eye.

Sometimes the blast leaves a corpse—a black hole a million billion times denser than gold. Or it leaves a "neutron star" spinning like a teacup. (The revolutions are timed in milliseconds.) Sometimes a supernova not only blows off its own material but also bulldozes a canal through the rest of its galaxy. Gravity reclaims the gusher while the galaxy's still siphoning into it, and you can see in pictures the stream of interstellar gas and dust bent back like a shower from a hose. Evolution hardwires us to stroll through this kind of violence like soccer revelers, compose a little night music, make ourselves at home. We're totally, miraculously insane.

Astronomers aren't so different from anyone else. Maybe a little more eclectic. They believe firmly in the existence of ETs—just by law of averages, given the size of the universe. They have little doubt that the dinosaur Ice Age was brought about by meteors. "One asteroid in the nineteen-eighties actually passed between the moon's orbit and the Earth," Phillips said. "Though people didn't realize it until afterward." (Another near miss was reported the next month.) "It's only through the use of spy satellites designed to monitor nuclear testing that people have started to see how common these things are."

"It's probable that one reached the Earth near Russia," Suntzeff said. "There's an area where all the trees were blown down and stripped of their branches."

I asked if any of this made the universe seem less benign to humans somehow.

Phillips laughed. "I don't know. I guess ever since I've studied science I've come more to understand that we're just a tiny part of it all. Things are inevitable, and it's neither good nor bad; it's just what it is. Though it's certainly beautiful."

"What intrigues me," I said, "is how we've developed this answering capacity to respond to the beauty of it."

"Even more so for us as astronomers," Phillips said, "in that we're privy to information most people don't really have. Most people haven't really seen the Milky Way. Well, we've seen it hundreds of times, and we know exactly what it is. It blows me away every time I look at a map of the sky. So we have an appreciation for the complexity and the immensity of the universe that many people don't have. I think many people would be frightened by it."

"And you're not?" I said.

"The Christians say God has an overall plan—and men say, 'All right, in the end it'll all be cool, because if we do good works and believe in God we're all going to go to heaven.' And that allows us to face death—as well as other things that are difficult to understand. Like, why does a child get leukemia at the age of five? Personally, I think why this child got leukemia is there's a physical explanation for it. Maybe a gamma ray came through the atmosphere at some time and altered his cells. But I know that's a cold way of looking at it. And I'm sure on my deathbed I'll be as afraid of dying as anyone else."

You can think and think about the universe and never get anywhere. But you can also see it everywhere you look. You can see the universe crush Robert De Niro into penitent sobs in *The Mission.* You can see Louis Armstrong hold the universe together with a note.

Cosmologists, of course, take these phenomena literally—playing them back a frame at a time, trying to find the hidden strings. There's a cockroach-like tenacity to cosmology, matching the shadow dance of the universe step for step, holding all its mysteries to be knowable. And cosmology may be right. The old sensation of a magical, inscrutable heavens may finally be just a lie my genes have told to help me sleep. Or it may be a deep awareness that science is the height of human folly, that you could club the stars to death and never scratch the consciousness beneath them. Though you can't help marveling at science for trying.

For instance—and I've stopped trying to understand this—though the laws of physics and math fall apart at the level of quantum particles, cosmologists aren't discouraged, because it all works out, awfully close anyway, if you theorize that the universe is woven out of tiny existential loops. (There isn't even Nothingness between them—the loops *define* space.) Or possibly there are separate, impervious bubble universes, one for each incompatible system of math.

Then there is the Theory of Inflation, which says that a whole slew of longstanding conundrums is explained if you add a little wrinkle to the Big Bang—the cosmos just had to leapfrog conventional math to morph disproportionately from virtual nothingness to the size of a grapefruit in the first 1,000,000,000,000,000,000,000,000,000,000th of a second. Cosmology will work this all out yet.

But there was not much happening right that minute, that night, with the galaxies drifting by and the universe buoyant, all its balls in the air, like Mary Tyler Moore's flung hat. And us scavenging around below in the weird calm mirth of the freeze-frame, keeping our spirits up. We decided maybe to drop in on the facility's other domes. We bopped over dirt lots, dangling our penlights in blackness outside. The visiting astronomers were at keyboards, pondering next moves over blinking cursors.

I shook hands with a kid named Chris, part of a Harvard study of the southern skies. He was trying to see if you could account for the gravity that brought galaxies together into clusters, and he was trying to do this without relying on the theory of dark matter—which essentially explains any missing gravity by giving it a name. "And that doesn't feel good," Chris said. He was young, athletic-looking, and respectful in a way that wiped the last exultant strains of classic rock right out of Phillips's night. Phillips warned him: "I used to look like you."

Soon we were plodding back to the 4-meter dome, past billions and billions of stars, not even looking up. At 5 a.m., Infinity is annoying. Phillips looked for any good e-mail and found Mike Fennel's. Fennel requested Phillips's help ("as this is a very low-budget experiment") in relaying tether-viewing coordinates to Alan Dressler at Las Campanas. I lingered at the coffeemaker, weighing a packet of Boldo tea, then thought better of it.

The verdict on the latest supernova, as dawn approached, was that it was still getting brighter. It conformed more with each day to one set of supernova precursors, and less to certain others—in its small way, this was influencing the cosmic debate. Three weeks later I'd get a summary from Phillips by phone. The supernova, he said, maxed after four more nights. The European prediction scored a bull's-eye; Phillips was three days off.

In terms of the supernova survey, the universe was still entirely a battleground. "If we simply assume that all supernovas have the same intrinsic luminosity, then we confirm Sandage's answer for the Hubble constant: about fifty-three or fifty-four," said Phillips. "But if we factor in our observations that say there's a relationship between how fast a supernova fades and what its luminosity is, then we get a slightly larger value, something in the mid to high sixties." This translated to a 15-billion-light-year universe—a universe younger than some of its oldest stars. A nonsense universe.

The result had provoked an unhappy letter from Sandage. "It's not definitive, and it's only a twelve percent difference," Phillips said. "But it's not in the fifties, where he likes it."

Allan Sandage died in 2010. In 2014, most scientists concur that the constant is indeed in the neighborhood of seventy: in-betweeny, unromantic—the kiss of a sister.

But the SEDS-2 space tether was a nice little wonder to behold. We very nearly missed it. We barged outside at the appointed moment, forgetting penlights and binoculars and stopwatches; we had to rush back in to fill our pockets with these things. At last we were perched on the edge of the mountaintop, facing south and talking low with a few more bodies trotting toward us from the other dome. The sky was black, and the constellations held us in their focus. We settled in.

When it appeared at 5:32, it was so close and clear it seemed phony. "Here it comes—wow," Phillips said. It resembled a puppet that had been shot from a cannon. The head was a white bulb, and it had a tail as long as the width of the moon and bent straight down, which seemed odd; it whizzed straight toward us like a line drive—I felt myself digging in to break one way or the other. Then it was straight overhead, and then past us, and we were searching ourselves for those stopwatches and penlights, beating our coat pockets like guys on fire.

It took the astronomers days to piece together what happened in half a minute—how the sun, on the brink of rising, illuminated the polyethylene strand. How a collision with space dust must have clipped off two-thirds of its length. All this was explainable in retrospect, but while I was actually watching the tether, I felt like anything was possible. I felt nervous and happy-footed at the same time, and I kept worrying that I could have been beaned. I had the sensation that there was some instinct of apprehension inside of me that could take the measure of space the way an animal measures a leap.

There at the bottom of the world or at the end of it, a lot of scientists believed that this sensation could be expressed in the form of a number. A few, like Allan Sandage, insisted that the number had been found. Within twenty years, Phillips and Suntzeff assured me, the question of the age, size, and fate of the universe would be closed.

7

Consider the Richardsons

A year before I married the kind of religious Christian who believes that the whole Bible is God's inerrant word—including those lines commanding wives to submit graciously to husbands—I remember praying, with the sincerity that comes from real selfishness, for God to send a godly Christian wife. This even despite the fine print of the next verse, commanding the husband to lay his life down for his partner the same way Christ laid his life down for the church. Every man secretly dreams of doing something like that anyway, for a woman who won't laugh at him for trying. Not that I thought it was possible to do so and still fit anywhere in my old world, and the future would tell.

But it was a time for vulnerability and dreaming. I was divorced six years from Tara, with a seven-year-old son. She was a former B-movie actress I'd waited years to catch in a vulnerable moment, which hadn't proved a strong foundation for a marriage. By 2000, at age forty-five, I was laid up half a year on my sofa from a basketball injury on Valentine's Day, having tried to keep up with men half my age after sending unwelcome flowers to an estranged girlfriend who was younger than the men. I'd never belonged to a church, even though in my part of the world a drive up Palo Verde Avenue toward the town of Bellflower was like a film loop of churches interrupted by parks. I may have been ready for a right-hand turn.

My image of a Christian single until then was Kelly, who was sexy and untouchable and would listen to music in your bedroom but not dance, even though she knew that you knew she could dance. She moved away to Santa Barbara (almost overnight, on a vision) and rented a maid's quarters there, working as a secretary for a church. A couple of times I drove up and said hi, both of us pretending it wasn't far out of my way, but we finally lost touch. She was damaged, like me, like a lot of people who come to God, but she had a raucous free laugh that feared no one, and she was chastely touched by my horny crush on her, a response too knowing and gracious to have come from any of the women I used to date in those days. Implicit in her self-control, even to an outsider like me, was the dream that if you married her she'd be wholeheartedly yours.

If God is who he claims to be, then any prayer starts out selfish in the deepest way: the ugliest truth about you becomes your most genuine offering, a finger painting in blood and jam. If we were such excellent people on our own, we wouldn't need him to be Him. Of course, I was praying to be a gift to my partner, too—but I didn't kid

myself that my generosity matched my want. No one whose
family history inspires any faith in marriage bothers to pray
the way I prayed. My whole motive was my belief that with
a godly wife I was less likely to be abandoned or mutilated
or betrayed, and the other particulars were fluff: that she
would be a Daughter of the King, sewing curtains out of
bedsheets, lovely in sandals, laughing at days to come—
details I got from the Book of Proverbs, the Song of
Solomon, and a Christian self-help book on how to save
your marriage by prayer, which someone had pressed upon
Tara right before she divorced me. So I wrote down and
folded into my wallet this request for a partner and a play-
mate, a fitting word choice after an adolescence shaped by
Hugh Hefner.

As it happened, Kriss pedaled up on a bike at a yard sale
and made friends (she says she had a Mountaintop
Moment, halfway between premonition and déjà vu). A few
weeks later, we discovered, to our stupefaction, that *she was
the acquaintance who'd loaned my former wife that book.*

She'd tried to be an angel, in other words, then lost her
own husband to cancer after they'd had two children in
three years, and for the first six months of dating her, I was
brilliantly reluctant: *Who wanted the baggage?* But what I
have to tell here is how grateful I was soon after, not only
for the cosmic coincidence of meeting and marrying the
marriage-book girl, but also for being unashamed to jump
at it—for being impoverished, essentially, and letting myself
be rescued from a divorced dad's shitty excuse for a life. It
would be my desert island book, this *Love Life for Every*

Married Couple; marriage being to me the most obvious path to the hardest lesson we've all got to learn—how to love another human—with all other roads leading backward to dust.

It changes something when you open yourself to the proposition that lines in the Bible about becoming One Flesh are not just metaphor. On our honeymoon, not the first night but close enough, my wife examined my body both for erogenous zones and cancerous moles; I'd been married before, and it wasn't like that. Early on, wounded by her lukewarm approval of my writing, I announced that I was done opening up "that area of my life" to her, provoking what in her eyes amounted to a spiritual emergency, a foothold for the devil to divide us.

Later, I got water baptized at her church's Wednesday night Power Encounter, a public declaration of my inward decision, holding both sides of the tub as if I were waiting for the thrill ride to begin.

A couple of times Kriss and I made love with such triumphant friendship and security that it seemed like another species of sex altogether, one nonstop affirmation building to orgasm—momentarily peeking into the garden of freedom and trust that partners without long rambling sexual pasts must take for granted. (We wondered; we asked.)

Before I got engaged, an editor friend had told me that none of her married friends seemed happy, and I told her that all the marriages in my neighborhood seemed perfectly happy, as long as the husband was conservative and workaholic. I only meant it to be provocative, but part of me believed it. All my images of marital harmony (whether fifties-stoical or modern-liberated) involved giving up the fantasy of having your deepest needs met. At the same time, I was encountering a community of born-again types who believed they were the real feely progressives, because they *hadn't* given up on the opposite sex, and because they believed in being more intimate rather than less. The buzz-word about marriage in my wife's church was *accountability*. Men were accountable (both to their wives and other men) for "unclean thoughts," women for "hardened hearts" and "critical spirits." Saving each other from error was a sacred duty (from scripture: "speaking the truth in love"). Being a doormat by self-sacrifice was a pejorative, but only barely.

I met the Richardsons at the Long Beach Christian Fellowship family Christmas celebration, with Doug the pastor-husband beaming from the piano and Valerie, his wife, leaning forward in a velvet chair with her ankles crossed and a children's storybook in her lap. In what I thought was going to be a receiving-line encounter—an occasion to drop off a business card and leave—I told Valerie I wanted to write a magazine piece about the daily struggle of a literalist, Bible-based Christian marriage, how life is for the sort of couple who would as soon die as broach the subject of divorce. She said, "Oh, how nice," but dropped the subject immediately to welcome me and ask about me and tell me all the nice things she had noticed about my son. We didn't do the interviews until nine months later.

Doug Richardson wears a square-bottomed plaid shirt, roomy jeans, and loafers, with a cell phone on his belt. His full head of evangelical hair is brown and groomed back in the style of a count. The unlined face and sloping shoulders create an almost disturbing posture of exposure, halfway between Richard Nixon and Andy Kaufman, as though he were standing all alone beneath a shower. That is the slouch he assumes on stage Sunday mornings when he's waiting to sing a new song to the Lord.

Valerie wears a black V-neck over prewashed jeans and is almost too thin, with the haunted, waifish beauty of a seahorse. Her voice is soothing, and she has a deep gallows laugh. When Doug was a nerdy twenty-year-old music minister and saw her picture in the wedding album of a friend, she was a new believer and wore her hair in a feathered shag like Karen Carpenter. She must have made an impression in a bridesmaid's dress, because he went home and told his parents he'd just seen the woman he would love for the rest of his life. Thirteen days later he proposed, acting on the courage to make himself a prophet or a fool.

At the time, Doug Richardson was not only a virgin but had never had a girlfriend. From these facts, his parents derived that he meant business. "My mom and dad knew that kind of thing had never come out of my mouth, and they also knew they had a pretty strange kid."

Whereas Valerie was a woman with a past. Drugs, already married and divorced, and then Jesus.

Doug says, "My parents' big concern was: Is she a woman that really loves God, and how do we know that? And I said, Mother, I heard her pray."

He brought a Dutch apple pie on his first visit to her house for tea. The next week, not to be outdone, Valerie made filet mignon and served it on her mother's fine china. Their first restaurant was the El Torito in Huntington Beach, where Valerie disclosed her pre-religious wildness, not as any apology, and they cried. After two abortions and a divorce, she had followed the newly saved ex-husband to church. There a youth pastor looked in her eyes with a hand on each shoulder and repeated, so many times Valerie says she lost count, *You are a child of the living God.* "I wasn't sharing this with Doug out of shame—I knew what God did for me on the cross," she says. "I'm not second class in his kingdom in any way. But I wanted to make sure that Doug understood."

Besides which, she thought he was a prince, with life in his eyes and a love for the Lord. They drove to Long Beach's Terrace Theater, for the terrace, where they strolled with Valerie's arm inside Doug's, because she cut the inexperienced man a break and put it there.

Not that Doug Richardson was sinless. "I brought patterns of self-hatred—inward things," he says. "Some men's sins, like the Bible says, are obvious, while the sins of others trail behind them. I didn't actually do all the things that she'd done, but there were insecurities that were just as destructive, ways I rejected myself."

Valerie's nature had been to shut down under stress or interrogation. Doug was a lifelong verbal processor. ("The poor woman," he says devoutly. "The. Poor. Woman.") They also had culture clash to overcome. Years into their marriage, when they saw a man smoking a joint, Valerie had to tell Doug what it was. After a Christmas dinner where one of Valerie's relatives, then addicted to drugs, slumped half-consciously onto a couch, Doug refused to accept the possibility that the man was loaded. "But honey," he explained to her, "it's *Christmas!*"

On the other hand, what good was purity if it wasn't fanatical? There was more to lose than gain, for example, by exposure to popular culture. *Schindler's List* was an important movie, so they took themselves and their teenaged sons to see it. But Valerie shielded Doug's eyes at his own request from the scenes of violence and sex, because he knew the obsessive power of images in his head.

Why the most conservative evangelical churches in America always look the least sacred is, to anyone unfamiliar with Protestant history, one of God's abiding mysteries. Doug Richardson's explanation sounds as reasonable to a new Christian as any: God's forever appearing in new forms. Which is why every few Sundays he turns the stage over to a worship band in Generation Y packaging (droning, acoustic), then courageously defends them against the intolerant spirits in the audience, who in reality are nowhere to be seen.

Afterward, people mingle in the foyer where clannish

banners hang and the bulletin board announces prayer meetings and Bible studies with names like "Ignite," "Turning Point," "Fresh Fire," and, for kids K–5, "Diggin' Deeper." Almost everyone of age is married (does domesticity lead to the harder drug of religion, or vice versa?), and a lot of the congregation's roofers and floor guys and dry-wall contractors helped build the church itself, a block from the Long Beach Airport and across from a place that either produces or disposes of tufts and tumbleweeds of shredded aluminum.

Although Doug's verbal manner always snaps back to cerebral, he preaches a message that is decidedly anti-intellectual (the theme of an upcoming men's outing is torn between paintball and indoor rock climbing), a style so fixed within evangelical politics that the Christian right famously tried to embrace born-again Jimmy Carter, who opposed them on almost everything, and distrusted Ivy League Episcopal George Herbert Bush, who agreed with them nearly across the board. By affiliation, the Long Beach Christian Fellowship is nondenominational charismatic, by way of the Pentecostals, who take their name from the biblical ingathering of believers so passionate with the Holy Spirit that onlookers concluded they were drunk. Both Doug and Valerie graduated from King's Seminary in the San Fernando Valley, whose online mission paragraph uses the term *Spirit-filled* three times. The Pentecostal litmus test of talking in tongues—unchallenged at LBCF but not really talked about, practiced politely in the spaces of songs—grew from historical events just up the 710 Freeway (the 1906 flowering of the Holiness Movement, the 1961 glossolalia of a Van Nuys minister), a context that asks you to look twice at stucco-dwelling California and believe that God chose this place for a "mighty unfolding," as the Richardsons thought in the 1980s and still do.

For their marriage, the Bible laid the challenge out neatly. Foremost, they were to "cleave to one another." ("Anything that is a secret for you can be enjoyed in private, and this is what we are trying to do away with," reads an advice column in *Christianity Today,* titled "Why Affairs Happen.") They were to leave their mothers and fathers for marriage, wives submitting graciously to the decisions of their husbands, husbands submitting selflessly to the happiness of their wives, and then a couple lines later each submitting "one to another," a confusion that could drive anyone to Jesus. They were to be patient and kind and keep no record of wrongs, a text familiar to anybody who's ever attended a wedding of any kind, with the difference being that to the Bible-based Christian, it is a litmus test for salvation.

One day, Doug tried to drag Valerie out of bed for a morning devotion. She gave him a look, and he backed off. The next day it occurred to him to prop her up with pillows and hand her a Bible and coffee and give her forty-five minutes to herself. "Churches were emphasizing order and structure," he says, "and we tried." She was working a swing shift after caring for their two small boys during the day. Doug needed to leave early to work at an aircraft facility, and morning was their only chance to pray as a couple.

The morning devotional never took in a formalized way. Instead, prayer became their background music. "We walk now at night," Valerie says. "Sometimes we walk and talk, and sometimes we walk and talk and pray."

But it seemed like a shaky start, with altars exploding all around them. "I remember Doug trying to Teach Us Around the Table." Valerie's laugh lets you know where this idea went. "The boys had little workbooks they had to do."

Doug's face is so non-contesting, she hurries to soften the joke. "It was sweet! But it wasn't really . . . *inspirational,*" she says, and her tactfulness nearly gives way to laughter again.

Because they were obedient, God liked calling into question things they thought they knew, to show them that He was bigger than any preconception. Sometimes they would fight, and the fights seemed to get worse for a while. One time, inevitably, Doug pulled out Paul's epistle to the Ephesians and said, "I'm the head—*submit.*" And Valerie said, "No, no, you have to earn it." He'd pulled what was a trump card in their church, and she ripped it up, and they had to start again, broken before God.

I liked hearing how they weathered their fights. One recent morning Doug jumped on Valerie for "rescuing" a manipulative congregant, and Valerie jumped on Doug for barfing up her history as a rescuer—"And I feel like I've come a long way, baby, from that history"—all before breakfast.

Doug: I eventually said, "Do you see how it could have sounded to me like you were rescuing?" And Valerie said, "Yes, I could see that."

Q: What do you do in the middle of a fight?

Doug: It depends. When you've been married for twenty-three years, you don't have to be that skilled to decide where to go for dinner. But when you have a major conflict, that's where you've got to have the goods. I would say in the first twelve, thirteen, fourteen years, we went into breakdown fairly often. [*Breakdown* is terminology from Breakthrough Training, a Christian relationship seminar developed in Santa Rosa, California.] Sometimes we would walk out of the room.

Valerie: Raise our voices. Or want to shut down.

Doug: The typical thing. I'd get mad, and as I'd go out the door—you know what I'm going to say.

Valerie: He starts thinking about me.

Doug: I'd end up shopping for her, buying her a card to make up.

Valerie: And I'd end up getting a call from his cell phone.

Doug: She always did have the capacity to stay mad longer.

Valerie: That's a terrible thing.

Doug: It got her nervous, though, after a few years, when she noticed that I was starting to stay mad longer.

Valerie: It was what I'd been sowing into the relationship.

Doug: But that's not the pattern today.

Valerie: I think one of the most wonderful tools we have—and I have to give Breakthrough credit for helping clarify this whole concept—is to ask yourself in the middle of conflict, what are you "committed to cause" for the other person? What do you want them to experience? Are they getting your heart? Because sometimes people get our words, but they don't get our heart.

Doug: That's the difference between being right and being authentic.

Q: Does the other one ever not *want* your heart?

Doug: I remember her being madder than a pistol one day, and in the midst of the altercation I realized: she's pissed off, and I've caused this. She is ready to jump off a cliff. She is gone. She is Done With This Conversation. I remember taking hold of her arm and begging her, please, give me another chance. Let's go again.

Valerie: Stay in it.

Doug: Please, don't ditch the conversation. I know you have every reason to. Let's just see if we can get through this.

Valerie: He salvaged that episode.

Doug: That's because she got my heart. At that volatile point, she could tell: he's getting that he's been a jerk. And we finally turned it around.

Q (to Valerie): What about him not wanting *your* heart?

Valerie: He doesn't get *angry* angry. I've seen him *angry* angry less than half a dozen times. And then it's like [deeply feminine regret, as though she'd accidentally launched a nuclear missile]: Oh, my. This isn't good. This is very bad. He's never been violent or anything like that, but there have been times when I knew he was very angry, and [mortified laugh] I was the cause of it. But he was very forgiving when I came to that realization.

Early in my marriage to Kriss I got jealous. When she talked to other men, she made deep, deep eye contact and was never the first to walk away, despite crying children, raised eyebrows, sulking guests. She either knew nothing about how men read women, or knew all about it and enjoyed the attention, an accusation I longed to make if I could do so without appearing . . . jealous. When I tell my life story, I can make it all about people leaving, people being left, people lashing out in fear of being left. The Richardsons respond to this confession by barely comprehending. Once, Doug told me, Valerie got hit on by the neighborhood mechanic, and afterward Doug corrected her in love—not for flirting (she hadn't), but for missing the spiritual opportunity to tell the mechanic his disrespect of her marriage didn't flatter him or her.

Falls from grace are everywhere. First there were the Bakkers, and then Jimmy Swaggart, straying onto the gravel motel parking lot of the heart, and then it was Jane Fonda, dropping Ted Turner for not following her into the Bible, perhaps failing to find the just-right scriptural self-reproach ("Be submissive to your husbands so that, if any of them do not believe the word, they may be won over without words when they see the purity and reverence of your lives"). The evangelical recording industry is an inferno all its own. Amy Grant divorced Gary Chapman, the host of Prime Time Country. Sandi Patty married backup singer Don Peslis, with whom she'd been having an affair. All told,

Christian divorce is as common as secular divorce, with the adultery rate among pastors in ministry a weirdly impressive 23 percent (*Christianity Today*).

The Richardsons do not run from these hissing grenades so much as stride right through. "I can't believe it's true among real believers," Valerie says. It is her turn in this marriage to be incredulous. She is thumbing my copy of the *LA Weekly* from the back, innocently encountering twenty pages of sex ads, which in Doug's office recede as if through the wrong end of a telescope. To Doug's mind, sexual "brokenness" (as he considers everything from homosexual attraction to hetero porn) is everywhere, largely the church's fault for not addressing it. God has given him either the courage or the tone-deafness to speak such thoughts with absolute serenity (he'd preached on masturbation one infamous Easter, the sanctuary filled with everyone's visiting friends and family). He himself had been molested by a relative in his childhood; he'd done some work at becoming unreachable by shame.

"We live at the far end of the openness spectrum," he says. "How many times a day do we say, *a penny for your thoughts?*"

A turning point, back before openness became intolerably necessary, was when Doug returned with Valerie from vacation to find a message from his best friend, the music pastor, confessing that he'd been hiding an affair. (Always the music pastor.) Two prominent couples were destroyed, and the congregation was in chaos, weeping and blaming; Doug continued preaching for a few weeks, having been struck somewhere between the shoulder blades, less advancing really than falling forward. He may not have been the most intimate fellow in the world (it seemed to signify something that his closest friend had never hinted about a problem), but no one ever said he wasn't sensitive. For a few months he shut down, making everything worse. Finally he agreed with Valerie to have dinner at the Belmont Brewing Company with a couple who'd gone through Breakthrough Training and knew all the lingo, the sort of couple who, when you confessed what you were doing, would respond, "Is it working?"

Valerie went to Breakthrough first, where she says she learned to "experience the way others experience you." She did this because relationships were the most important thing in life ("How can you say you love God whom you don't see, when you hate your brother whom you do see?"), and what turned Doug around was that later, during his depression, she made a stand. They were driving to minister to a congregant, and he didn't know if he could make it to the door. He said, "Honey, I believe that you love me more than anyone on earth. And I believe that God hears prayers of love. Would you put your hand on my heart and pray for me?"

She put her hand on his heart and prayed, and he had "a physical manifestation. I felt strengthened in my body, and I was strengthened for the next two weeks while I was waiting to go to Breakthrough in Nashville. We know—I'm certain—I would never have got on the plane."

She also assured him he was more important to her than

the church or what they did—a standard of self-sacrifice Doug began prescribing to husbands at LBCF by telling them they would reap from marriage as they sowed. For a time, men cringed when he rose to the pulpit. Once, he directed couples to study a series of videotapes and books by the Christian relationship guru Gary Smalley, whose foundation for marital therapy is summarized in the all-capitals axiom: IF A COUPLE HAS BEEN MARRIED FOR MORE THAN FIVE YEARS, ANY PERSISTENT DISHARMONY IS USUALLY ATTRIBUTABLE TO THE HUSBAND'S LACK OF APPLYING GENUINE LOVE.

Wives who hadn't been loved properly by their parents may be "difficult to deal with," Smalley acknowledged to men, but this was an academic qualification, because "biblically speaking, you're still responsible for the disharmony in your home"—the sort of Promise Keepers riff that, depending on whom you ask, either sugarcoats sexism or creates a booby-prize authority that only a man could want.

Doug Richardson is serene on this question, in a Christian sex-ed way. "God has designed us physically so that men impart a seed and women receive it. And there's a mirror to that emotionally, which is that women are ready to respond, but men have to be ready to contribute love. And when that's absent, trouble ensues. Now, that's not just my opinion—that's twenty-five years of pastoral experience in listening to couples' stuff. Men are generally stupid, self-absorbed, and don't have a clue what a relationship is about. Most women want intimacy, and most men don't even know what it is. In our own marriage, there's no doubt that I've brought most of the chaos, the long-term stuff that weighs us down."

"It used to be that way," Valerie says. "We've switched."

In the past, after a fight, Doug used to worry Valerie might leave. Or, convinced no one could love him, he might say something preemptively harsh. But she'd call him on his put-downs, until he had no place to turn but to the proposition that a spouse was a sharpening stone. This was his prayer to God: "I'll go anyplace and do anything, I just want you to deal with this part of my life."

Sometimes the Richardsons sound like senior citizens though only in their forties, maybe because religion provides a shortcut to the kind of wisdom in which disappointment becomes the bread of contentment. Even the potential frills of religious marriage (the Bible says Doug's body belongs to Valerie and hers to him—is God sure?) are too deep to be strictly fun. To an outsider, all the misgivings are about the cost. I ask if it honors God to give yourself sexually if you aren't in the mood.

"Being in the mood has become such a mutual thing to us," Valerie says. "We become sensitive to each other's needs."

During one bad period, they were challenged to deal with sexual loneliness on account of Doug's rheumatoid arthritis. "It was all I could do to get through a day. Sometimes I'd have to stop my day and go home. And anything that wasn't a necessity was impacted."

"But I never felt detachment from him emotionally," Valerie says. "We kept connected largely due to his desire to know what was going on inside of me. I always felt we were intimately connected."

Inevitably, they've led Christian marriage retreats. These differ from the world of secular self-help somewhat in tone, though maybe not so much from *Cosmo,* addressing the opposite sex from a perspective of Care and Feeding. Partners are told to think up ways to "Meet Your Partner's Physical Needs" and "Increase Spontaneous Loving Acts," and "Support Him Through Loving Prayer." To close, there are romantic dinners with ceremonial recitals.

"I sang 'Unforgettable' to you," Doug remembers.

"Oh, you sang it to me, and Gail was singing it to Bill." Their friend Gail died of cancer not long after. "She had a beautiful voice. That was a great memory," Valerie says.

"Do you remember we were recarpeting the boys' room that night, and the sample we'd picked happened to be called 'Unforgettable'?"

Valerie's jaw drops. "How did you remember that!" she says.

"It was unforgettable!"

Doug is not a great funny man. He surprises himself too much.

Some of the Richardsons' marital recommendations evoke Dilbert's America: mission statements, Unified Visions. Each week, one spouse should say to the other: What is it we should want to accomplish?

"We take it right down to the practicalities," Doug says. "Not just, what am I doing or what are you doing? But is family the number-one thing? Do we want to call the kids and have them over for dinner? So we're actually doing things according to what's important, as opposed to being absorbed by being busy. When we let work or responsibilities dictate our lives, we're unhappy."

Vision-sharing, an obsession with translating prophesy into earthly detail, is important in the culture of LBCF. When a congregant says he wants to be more trusting of God or more honoring of his wife, the stock response is: "What would that look like?" One husband might commit to pursuing his wife by leaving her a note each day (God pushing him to grow; he hates writing). Another has agreed to purchase Internet software that will notify his wife where he's been online. That Doug leads and outdoes the flock in sheer zealotry is a running joke among some of these guys, who had to sit next to their own wives in church the Sunday Doug announced he was building Valerie a meditation garden in their side yard.

Small gifts and gestures are nice but less crucial from the wife. Asked to name a counterpart gesture from Valerie, one church elder winks, "She's lived with Doug."

Through all this, though, I felt I owed the Richardsons some explanation as to where my own marriage and religious life were heading; this proved difficult, because I frankly didn't know. I wanted my wife and me to be as married as the Richardsons, without having to *become* them— not that we could, but I was drawn. I was drawn. Aside from being beyond dubious that a loving God would demand celibacy from gays, I couldn't think of an interestingly hostile question to ask them. I was sad that however cleansed my baptized soul may have been, my life to date was not. And confronted by a certainty as hard-won and preserved as Doug Richardson's, I felt like a bit of a creep, I felt like hitting him, and then I knew that I also admired him, admired them both like the bride and groom on a cake, and this drama felt about as old as life.

I was someplace way upriver from my comfort zone—this was years before I found my own denomination, with its own nuanced beliefs about equality and sexual morality—and the dislocation was so thorough that the vista from my suburb in North Long Beach sometimes took on an aspect of time travel. The LBCF men's group would have said this was good, that it was natural the first fruit of prayer would be the demolition of my prejudices, the expansion of my world. Unless in the guise of a seeker I was really a chameleon, fodder for gangs and cults and whoever loved me most. In which competition Christ's sacrifice could be said to have effectively closed the bidding.

Not that religion itself is such a shocking development in midlife. But ultra-religion might follow, if you're sincere. You might read the Bible, asking God and only God to show you if it's all true and if you've been an ass. Prayer might become, to paraphrase William Temple, not the support to a life of action, but the whole point of life, which action tests. You might pray out loud with people on the phone and with guests over dinner, as I did, sometimes with such humble inspiration that we cried, other times so fraudulently that I broke into a sweat, certain that I had more of God in the old days when I was openly confused.

At the men's group, I was coached to make promises. I gave my wife the right to stop me in the middle of any argument if she didn't get that I was for her, and to demand humility from me whether she'd confessed her part of the problem or not. She played that card a couple of times. I went to Breakthrough Training. In one game involving a shipwreck, if you weren't voted a seat on the lifeboat (only three out of forty people survived), you had to shout dying words explaining to your family why. Whatever your excuses, it always came down to your altruistic passion for your loved ones not being convincing enough.

I did believe that God would have his way with my new family, and that as scary as the Bible was, it was a love story, holding marriage above virtually everything, blessing marriage to the point that there could be no such thing as a mistake in what God joined together—that to trade everything I valued for love would be to gain everything back and more. But frankly, I believed that when I was a nonbeliever, too. Bringing outlaw romantics full circle. The Richardsons as Bonnie and Clyde.

My marriage to Kriss would last ten years, until the damage done by selfish fear and disrespect outweighed the vessel's ability to contain it. But I do not believe today that either the divorce or my Christian marriage were a mistake. If that's playing both sides of the fence, so be it.

And I can picture the Richardsons still as they were on their first date at the Terrace Theater going safely, almost unfairly, in a swoon. If they were doing love and marriage all for themselves, you'd have had to hate them. Valerie liked to quote St. Peter: You've been blessed to be a blessing. "So if we do this, our marriage has a blessing quotient. Nonbelievers might be blessed by it."

"The bottom line," says Doug, "is that the cross has dealt our selfishness a death blow. Relationships don't work because people are selfish."

Maybe to challenge himself on that point, Doug lobbed a bombshell of gender equality at the congregation one fall, announcing that Valerie would be ordained co-pastor of the church. In some individual-snowflake way unique to the Richardsons, you could see this trying to happen—Doug the Pygmalion, both absorbed in his wife's untapped potential and fantasizing about an occasional breather from his role as the oddly cast patriarch. Nevertheless it was going to be a difficult sell. Paul's words in the Bible ("not suffer a woman to teach") seemed inconvenient to say the least, and for two straight Sundays the largely conservative congregation fidgeted and took notes while Doug turned academic, explaining the epistle to the Ephesians as a "contextual particularity," addressed to an earlier time when education had been limited to men.

The date arrived. Guest speaker Dr. Paul Chappel, King's Seminary, Who's Who in Religion, touched all the bases of the Richardsons' story: that they were called to the Lord, and then to each other, and then to Long Beach to do a new work. He traced the movement of the Holy Spirit through the history of the Pentecostal Charismatic movement (representing 530 million followers worldwide, Chappel claimed, two-thirds of those who newly come to the kingdom of God) to his own quickening that led him to call Valerie to head the King's Seminary Committee on Women in Ministry. He invited her up to the stage, and she sat down in that velvet chair in which no one reclines, hands folded over the book in her lap that this time was her Bible, the elders of the Long Beach Christian Fellowship surrounding her, hands laid on to pray, Doug standing nervous and proud.

And there things got confused: whether this was Valerie's ordination or Doug's retirement, whether he was empowering his wife or himself, whether she was fulfilling her destiny or his, whether one helping another ever failed to help oneself. "I get your heart," Valerie said to the congregation in Breakthrough language. "I get your love for me." Slowly at first but then heartily, Dr. Chappel spoke in tongues, a lot of people wept, adoring their royal couple, celebrating the Richardsons' marriage, and from the back of the room you could see the whole group around the couple, listening with heads bowed for a new word from God. Finally Doug released any parents in attendance to retrieve their children from Sunday school classes, because the praying was going to continue for a long time.

8

The Los Angeles
Writing Club

The Los Angeles Writing Club began just like a relationship—the small talk, the sharing of clever opinions while roaming wirelessly around the house, the panicked attempts to seem capable of interesting gossip. Later the instant intimacy, the thwarted infatuation, the hurt feelings, the prima donna desertions, and the interest waning like lust, all in a matter of weeks. But first the phone call. How would you like to write a new short story every two weeks, recapture all the vital hardship of writing without the material gain, and meet with a small group of strangers in order to take criticism? My conscience recognized the potential in this moment of truth. (Do you even remember why you first wrote? Is it all about the money then?) So I said yes to the Los Angeles Writing Club.

The sad fact was that I'd been wandering in a desert. I was feeling barren, even with Kriss pregnant and three children between us, and I was praying for money. Or, if necessary, a job. Twenty miles north of my neighborhood in Long Beach, the city of happy creatives shimmered. I could sense this reality just beyond my own reality, the way a lonely person knows it's date night outside.

To draw one more creative breath, writers always have to be falling in love with something or someone new. And spouses and friends hate us for that, even for confessing to our foolishness as if we secretly admire it. But foolishness in hard times truly is the heart of wisdom, because it always happens that not five minutes after you promise you'll say yes to anything, to get a teaching credential, to be a beginning writer again, the phone you were beginning to think was just a prop rings.

It was "Clive," a novelist—the British kind of novelist who always looks exhausted but never is, who sees fascinating paradoxes in every subject and explains them in an incisive, squishy-squeaky accent. Clive had been a fine chef and a classical guitarist before getting a quirky novel published the first time he tried. He was phoning from his house, a ghostly ruin in Koreatown with vines floating in the pool, which image placed him higher than me on several coolness measures at once. I saw him as one of those expatriate geniuses peculiar to Hollywood who acquire homes like they're birdbaths and romantically let them rot.

Now he was trying to recover the rhythm of writerly discipline. He had started the writing club almost on a lark—as if the bathroom mirror told him it was time to take up jogging. But in every other detail, he was almost amazingly formal. That title, for instance. The Los Angeles Writing Club. It could have been monumental arrogance or sober restraint or dumbbell English. But a British accent always gets the benefit of the doubt.

In response to a written protocol that would intimidate a proctor ("Each participant gets eight minutes, including questions to the writer and the reading of any excerpts . . . a timer will be used . . . revolving chair by alphabetical order . . . the onus of retaining focus is on the chair!"), the other four of us did the only thing we could do: We started exchanging self-deprecating e-mails, hoping to lower the bar. Or else that was just good manners on the part of "Macy" (a woman) and "Hollis" (her husband) and "Rhys"—all with genderless names from the right side of the tracks, the names of people who write wittier sentences on their coffee breaks than I do in three months at my desk. I would need to make them love me.

Then, just as quickly, I saw that I *could*. And they would make me love them too. We would be a boon to each other: made brave by discipline, made graceful, just flawed enough to have something to be graceful and brave about. Every blank page was a chance to redeem every ruined page that had ever come before. Which hints at why editors are able to manipulate writers into rewriting things over and over. They know we never stop hoping.

Without waiting a day, we set to work. The inaugural topic chosen by Clive—"My First Day at Harvard"— seemed uncannily fitting. Close to home. Inspired. Art imitating life. Form following content. I wanted to quit. Then came the writer's eternal fallback: Write about *that*. It might be my strong hand, disqualification. Don't let those brainy, legitimate writers drag you onto their turf.

Right there, a few theses began to fly. A dad in Long Beach walks with sack lunch to a bus stop for his first day at Harvard; he can't quite make connections on the Metro Rail and is back home by dinner. I didn't go with that premise—but there was something deeply true in the stranded emotion, as if I'd recurrently dreamed it. And aspects of it were all over the story I finally started (a doomed freshman arrives to find an overaged-male roommate diapering a baby; the two drink beer together by the Charles River and neither will last the semester; classes are missed and whole buildings not found).

This became my LA Writing Club routine: One afternoon for dreaming, another for speedwriting, and a third for turning that into readable sentences. Elatedly show the manuscript to my pregnant wife, whose face would confirm that the piece was unintelligible. Then edit through the night, completing in a day and a half what once would have taken me a month. I might have had my writing-club epiphany right there.

Even with Kriss in labor, part of me was with the group, whom I phoned from the hospital with the potentially ultimate excuse for bailing out (Benjamin, 7 lbs., 8 oz.). But I managed to e-mail them my story ahead of deadline and was proud of my devotion. I printed out the others' pieces, too, a neat, weighty sheath—fruition.

All these new soul mates to encounter through the medium of fiction. This was the courtship phase. Nobody had ever been us before.

Except for Rhys. Rhys's story was missing from the stack. I reread her e-mail.

Rhys, tragically, was leaving the Los Angeles Writing Club. Finished, overwhelmed, facedown at the first hurdle.

Hollis, an actor in his forties, was mainly in the group to be a good sport to his wife, and his strategy was to pad alongside her like Rocky Balboa keeping his girlfriend company at the ice rink. Hollis's first story was straightforward. The protagonist ruminated about majoring in environmental studies, and then he ruminated about young women's breasts—and now he had made it to Harvard, where a fellow could surround himself with both: sex and achievement. "And the future sure was looking good."

I reread his last sentence four or five times, rarely a good sign.

Terrified of finding nothing nice to say in a critique, I began looking for buried irony. Maybe, I wrote in my memo, the narrator's higher and lower natures had been vacillating. Maybe Hollis had been trying—not successfully, but ambitiously—to strike an exquisite tension between man's drive to be noble and his drive to get laid, never knowing which drive compensated for the other. Possibly this was satire, sending up the making of that stock American figure, the randy Congressman. It was all in there, somewhere. You could get some good ideas for stories from reading Hollis's stories.

Macy worked in talent management, and she was talented herself. Her piece was a sharp, lilting, funny-sad monologue full of dash and wit. A male narrator comes to realize that, having made it to Harvard, he is only trying to get even with the high-achieving girl who once dumped him, a wound that even Harvard will never heal. The story read like some of the best work of Lorrie Moore—you could feel the winning hurt in every laugh. Wow.

This guy Hollis did not deserve Macy at all.

Clive's piece could have been a lost draft of one of the *Best American Short Stories: 1942*—so entertaining and reader-friendly it seemed simply beyond our generation. There were pitch-perfect dialects, authentic locations, historical tidbits about philosophy and plumbing, and even an O. Henry twist. (The Harvard newcomer turns out to be the janitor.) The story's ending ruminated skillfully on the real purposes of philosophy, somehow marrying the story's practical and abstract layers without either getting in the way of the other.

At least that is the story Clive almost wrote. Because there were sloppy aspects, too—offhanded, as if Clive weren't really trying. Whole pages of dialogue were smushed together without paragraphing. End quote marks bumped into the next opening quote marks. And the crucial twist was detectable maybe a half-page too soon. Clive could have fixed all this in an extra half-hour or two. Why didn't he?

By week two, we had our own jokey tradition: that of the slightly hammy oral critique. Clive's delivery was part academic, part BBC entertainment anchor: He kept referring to the exotic setting of my Super Bowl story (for the assignment "The Bully Speaks") as "an American football match."

We were at Macy and Hollis's house in Fox Hills, with miles of Formica and great slab steppingstones and beams and light: an oasis with designer kitchens. The talented Macy had angel-fine red hair and marvelous freckly skin and wore cute Capri pants—a vision not of men's advertising but of women's. She was showing me the yard, because Hollis was still tapping away at the last of his critiques. Clive asked some interesting questions about the landscaping with his hands behind his back until Hollis emerged in a robe, papers flapping in one hand.

The narrator in my bully story was a new-breed football player who violently, remorselessly disgraced his aging opponent, one of the game's legendary gentlemen, on the field. Hollis dove right into his suave critique. "Right out of the bucket," he said, in a lusty cackle, "this guy grabbed me with his no-apologies philosophy."

He even read some of my lines out loud, passing them around like the most outrageous contraband.

"Folded over him like I was packing a bag!"

"Full beers flying!"

Then came Macy's crit: a deft, approving squeeze. She pointed out my story's "enchanting and manly phrases."

Two separate times, not to analyze this too closely, she interjected the stylishly potent dangler "Love it." Memorably: "I'm getting a feel for the Alan Rifkin style—love it." My own full name rubbing up against words like *feel, style,* and *love* is a sentence worth keeping, a sentence I would walk home to put under my pillow while forgetting my car.

We hit some trouble discussing Clive's piece. Which was a confusing development, because Clive's bully story, if possible, was even more virtuoso than his Harvard one. A philosophical joyride in the voice of a criminal psychologist who plumbs the heart of evil in a barroom after hours, it surpassed all of us, surpassed Mailer, surpassed De Lillo— all of us said so. But we confessed, too, that we had struggled just slightly to keep some of Clive's characters straight, because within the story, the characters themselves were telling a story. Which meant that there were quote marks within the quote marks. And all the quote marks were the funny British kind, so that the outside quotes were single ones, and the inside quotes were double ones. Clive had started the story, actually, with a triple inversion—in effect, a quoted quoted quote.

"How do you mean?" Clive said when we pointed this out.

"Well, the quotes within quotes," I said. "That, along with the British style—it just raised the level of difficulty for me. As a reader."

Clive tried to swallow this input. "I can't believe I'm hearing this."

We all searched ourselves. Hearing what?

He looked both betrayed and disbelieving. "I feel a little as if I were black and you'd called me a nigger," he said.

Macy and Hollis were having none of that. They stood their ground, firm and weary, as if pushing their drunken uncle back into his chair. And what happened to the onus of retaining focus? For I cite Clive: "It is not appropriate for the reviewed to interrupt . . . nor is it appropriate for other members of the group to interject. . . . On rare occasions, and then only unwillingly, the chairperson [on this night, me] may interrupt to keep focus or to arbitrate if the discourse becomes unruly."

But I got hamstrung by the literal text. How do you will yourself to interrupt "only unwillingly"? And whom to interrupt? Certainly not the aggrieved Clive. Instead I apologized—first for sounding culturally insensitive about punctuation (it was the first I knew that Americans could look down at the British), second for reading his story too fast (because all those quote marks were indeed in proper order). And we got through the calamity, confused, muttering, a small family of elephants soothing itself with rumbles eddying front and back. This brought us to Hollis.

Hollis this week had written a hard-knuckled story about the friendship between a schoolyard bully and the bully's protégé. Blood, fists, asphalt. The final paragraph closed with the bully ordering a strawberry parfait at an ice cream parlor and adding, as the waitress left the table: "With sprinkles."

Elated, I praised this new, nuanced, cryptic, almost-realized attempt at ironic swishiness, or swishy irony, or whatever it was. Only Hollis had no idea what I was talking about. No irony intended. No swishiness.

A total, awkward impasse. Finally I had to ask him outright. "Well, why did you write that then? About the strawberry parfait, and the sprinkles?"

And he said, completely puzzled, "Because that's what we always ordered!"

I phoned the next week to get the assignment for topic three. "Clive isn't going to make it this time," Hollis said.

That's too bad, I figured. We'll just set another date.

"No—I think Clive is done with the group."

Clive quitting his own group? That was troubling. (Could we survive leaderless? Could we keep that name?)

By cosmic coincidence, I had just been that week to Breakthrough Training—a la Doug and Valerie Richardson. It lasted four days. It was nearly sadomasochistic. In it, I learned that relationships were the most, if not the only, important thing in life. In other words, I was in a really good mind to admit wrongs, to salvage things. I would ask Clive what he needed in order to stay. I would do the humbling thing that allegedly would have salvaged a half-dozen important relationships, or marriages, in my past.

From the parking lot of the Seal Beach Pavilions, phoning in what looked a little like hurricane weather, I let Clive have his way. I let him prove, Socratically, that the rest of us could only have assailed his punctuation out of laziness, incompetence, or sheer dishonesty. Except one fragment of that concession just hung there in my throat—and I felt it necessary to point out to Clive there was such a thing as an honest mistake, and that if three readers of his story had made the same mistake independently of one another, it might be unloving if we didn't suggest, you know, that he take the information into account. On a final draft.

This set our phone call back to square one. So I prostrated myself all over again. After a half-hour of pleading, Clive said he'd think it over.

Then he called Macy and Hollis to tell them he was done with the group.

What the three of us did in the wake of this defection was reaffirm our vows. I did not want to squander the creative momentum, I said. The whole experience had been a small rebirth for me. I would stay devoted, even if it was just going to be me and the heartbreakingly talented Macy. And Macy's husband.

Belief in one another begat passion. Macy assigned a next topic, "The Comfort of Creatures," and I could feel claws and fur and mortality in it, all the sad gorgeousness of the fallen creature world. So I rose to the occasion, as did the others. The first sign that something magical had possessed us was a flurry of e-mails around 9 p.m. on the due date, warning each other that we were going to need every last minute to write.

I read Macy's story at midnight—slain by every word.

A story that could only be written by a certain kind of heartbreakingly talented woman with red hair, it told the fatal last ride and otherworldly release of Bo T. Blackeye: rodeo clown, widower, a man still leveled by the plain mention of a sentimental oak. ("Lily's oak.") Midnight felt like a new day starting.

"Are you coming to bed?" my wife asked.

I worked almost as hard on this critique as I had on my story:

Just as tragic and bowleggedly lyrical as a rodeo clown, in a voice I would follow anywhere, part Lorrie Moore (you really do have to read her) and part Mark Twain. The stoic nobility of Bo T.'s cowboy lonesomeness and low expectations is punctuated by attacks of sudden, doubled-over grief, which he wobbles through dutifully. ("Silly, he thought. Onward.") Such startling moments captured perfectly for me the phantoms of eternity that visit life on this side of heaven's reward, the life of anonymous heroes everywhere. . . .

Heroes like her.

And the only thing to do was to tell Macy so, honing my worshipful critique until nearly dawn. At which point, nearly hyperventilating over the page, I knew I would have to confess to my wife. The next day, in fact, I did so ("she's talented, and she really likes my writing, and—"). First giving myself an hour to end the literary romance in my head.

A relationship in Los Angeles ends just like a writing club. Or, say, beauty ("whose fair flower being once displayed, doth fall that very hour"), a metaphor Shakespeare made pretty but which Los Angeles perfected.

That next meeting had been a strong showing for all three of us. We really were continuing to improve. ("Creatures," I think, was my best story—I got the idea of writing about a trophy girlfriend torn between two guys and her preacher dad.)

Granted, Hollis's choice of a next topic was a little ominous ("The Last Call"). But I don't think that was the problem. The problem was something more mystical. The problem was that the whole summer seemed to turn like a sandstorm. An uncle of Macy's died, so she and Hollis had to drive up north. I took my family with newborn on a camping vacation. The club agreed on a two-week postponement—beware the single exception. Somewhere near Santa Cruz, I unfolded our assignment sheet once more and studied it.

"The Last Call" was a fertile enough subject. Maybe it could evoke a closing-time scene, like in Hemingway's "A Clean Well-Lighted Place." Or a boxing match, like in Jack London's "A Piece of Steak." Write about being middle-aged and punch-drunk, answering the bell of life when you can barely make out its sound any longer from the bells and birdies inside your head. Which brought up a few other associations—senility, vocation, maybe a combination of the two.

Between campsites I wrote down an idea: A police detective, well past retirement age, pores over phone records of a crime victim's Last Call. Trying to stay focused on what he's investigating, he regresses to an era when calls could be traced only by switchboards—a pre-digital era of innocence and neighborliness before all the rules changed and the child kidnappings began. Why was he in this house? What year was this? He couldn't remember. He needed to rest. He needed a cold drink. Hey. Was the murderer coming up behind him? No! That would be obvious, like Hollis. Or classical, like Clive. So what was wrong with obvious and classical? I wasn't sure anymore. I just knew that to make a suspense story with all the suspense perpetually squandered was a rare, possibly groundbreaking idea. I saw how all of life's memories would resound like dull gongs, how the house plan would be a labyrinth of lost youth, how the convolutions of Alzheimer's would be set against the timeless graveyard of the desert (the protagonist beginning to resemble the Harvard dad at the bus bench, maybe the same guy). I got home and wrote something elegiac instead of funny, and way too long, and it was only beginning. I wrote longer and couldn't remember why I began. Form followed content. Where was the magic? Deadline rolled around, and I was nowhere near completion.

That was okay with Macy and Hollis: It was a bad month for them, too. I should take my time, they told me. You see, they had a new puppy.

Yes? So? I had four children. Were they serious? Half of me was insulted, the other half grateful for the extension— my nobler and lower selves vacillating. My private eye was lost in a corridor. Now it was September.

My final voicemail from Hollis went like this:

"BAD DOG! BUSTER GET DOWN—Alan, sorry— I'm—BUSTER! GET! DOWN! I SAID: DOWN!—I'm going to have to—DOWN! GET! DOWN!—BUSTER!"

But even that shouting transmission seemed faraway

and fading. I was falling in love with fall now. Suddenly, I was getting paychecks and assignments—a miracle I credit, foolishly or not, to having taken chances for fun and for free. Like every other waste of time, in other words, this experience was worth the time. I believe Clive knew so when he felt moved to phone me in the beginning, whether Clive knew he knew it or not. So my wishing-well cosmos is intact.

As for the British novelist, the maiden, and the husband guy, I've started wondering: Were they real themselves or just characters? In the city of happy creatives, everything blurs. I only know that what felt charmed at the beginning of summer no longer was—inspiration's serial romance. I had flung myself at love and rebirth. I had three short stories, already garnering their murderously polite rejections from East Coast magazines. (This isn't for us. Thanks all the same. We'll pass.) I had given my heart, gone to Harvard and been back by supper, and the future sure was looking good.

9

Thin Ice

You have to imagine: This was five thousand years before today. This may have predated the wheel. When men didn't mourn the men they once were. When men were busy hunting to survive.

To think about Ötzi the Iceman's life was to hear the drumbeat of a Marine Corps commercial, to see the world through infrared crosshairs. "I guess the guy decided it was just too hard, so he threw in the towel," a salesman in a gun-and-archery store wisecracked to me. "*The way people do nowadays.*"

So with only a little trepidation I fantasize myself to the edge of the glacier where the Iceman died—see rock piles of color, a shivering marmot, the frost of my own breath—and something tells me when I get there that this is not a foreign place, that this is like my own world, only more real, that this is what life is made of, underneath. And maybe at bottom I'm courageous, resourceful; I'm part of everything.

I scrape arrowheads with antler tips, pack provisions wisely, make friends with existential fear. I wouldn't have done too badly here.

Or, I might have done horribly—blubbered for help, fumbled flints into the snow, toppled through ice like a tourist backing over a manhole. The Iceman may have done any of those things. History says to every sprawled corpse: Pretty nice try. The lab photos were impressive that way.

In the first one he looked like roasted turkey, but angrier. The fanged grimace, fists clenched. The protest of the arms. In shots released later—excavation shots—he seemed awash in glacial sorrow. The arm flung across the brow. He resembled somebody sobbing on a bar top. The trouble was almost too huge to name. He had wanted everything that would be possible someday, but not this day. He had wanted to visit a million unreachable places. He had delusions of passing for one of us. That was the way it had been for him, ever since *go,* ever since stereo vision replaced smell. The bola. Corded ware. The atlatl. Fire makers, socketed gouges, chisels, paring knives, all the iPhones of his day. And then he had gathered his nerve and lunged toward us, and in another fifty millennia the Austrians found him.

You also have to imagine, an ocean plus a continent away, my then-fiancée, Tara, the former B-movie actress, reading the *Los Angeles Times* and drinking coffee with her mom at their breakfast table/nerve center.

Before people lived their lives on screens, newspaper reading was actually an attractive calling, and somebody should have paid Tara to do it. More than anything, Tara loved the science pages: the reports about black holes and particle accelerators, anything liable to vindicate her conviction that the universe was more eccentric, and more forgiving of eccentric forces, than bullies and conformists and corporate capitalists had expected. I continuously got story ideas from Tara, including this one, because she was curious. Years later, she would be a fulltime caretaker both to her mother and to two special-needs children, and I still believe it isn't fair that she, and people like her, don't get rich.

On the other hand, she was susceptible to panic—a person who'd once halted a ride at Knott's Berry Farm on takeoff by the quality of her screaming. Had I not seen this happen, I would never have believed it possible.

I was more adventurous, but in a dilettante's way. I was starting to write for a magazine that would send you anywhere. I had written an article on rock climbing, and I could be fierce, throwing and slapping my limbs to get up the rock face, so focused I didn't know that my knees and shins were bruised and bleeding. People climb rocks over and over to stay close to that level of single-pointedness, but I wanted nothing more to do with it. The world-famous rock climber I'd been interviewing said, "You want to do it again, right?" And I said, "No. I don't."

After Tara and I were married, I got myself stranded on the roof one day without a ladder—I wasn't being paid to write about that—and she stood in the backyard becoming hysterical, because I'd decided it wouldn't hurt me to jump from there so long as I rolled with the fall, like Batman. We compromised. She dragged our mattress from the bedroom, a precaution I rolled my eyes at, but honestly it was fine with me. It was important to me to be married to someone more frightened of heights than I was. I've had it the other way around, and that wasn't so good.

When a middle-aged Nuremberg couple spotted the body in late September 1991, they first mistook it for a mannequin, then realized, "*Das ist ja a Mensch!*" It was trapped to its shoulders in rock-candy ice, jutting forth like the nose of a surfboard. A sort of squeaky, overspirited rescue effort took shape—mashing the crevice with ski sticks, cranking the body back and forth by one arm—during which Reinhold Messner, a world-famous mountain climber, literally strolled by.

Messner gave a very good showing of himself. He was the first to insist the body might be very old, and when Tirolean newspapers named him the discoverer, he graciously passed credit to the German couple, who sued the Austrian government two weeks later for half the royalties to all future exhibitions.

Newspaper artists struggled the most to depict him. Some drew him as Ivanhoe, not a wrinkle in his clothes; others had him low-browed and drooling, mouth open in primitive moral outrage, like Pete Rose. Lost-relative hunters turned up: People pointed at news photos of the noseless, Munch-like skull and gasped, "God, it's George." By December, when I arrived, the compulsion to relate had overflowed. The University of Innsbruck was surrounded by news crews, unreachable by car. The scientists huddled in the anatomy department, a den containing a stuffed boar, a row of skulls painted like beer steins, and a collection of lamps with bases made of lacquered organs.

From these scientists I learned that some mummies hold together less handsomely than others, depending on moisture. I learned that glacial tides often stretched corpses out like taffy with their arms over their heads, and other times shredded them completely. The university had recently fished two passengers from a car that plunged into a frozen lake in the 1930s; bacteria devoured the male driver, but above the waterline, perfectly muscled and placid as a doll, sat a waxed female, a famous skier whom the coroner wouldn't identify, apparently because she shouldn't have been with the driver. A former owner of the Hollywood Wax Museum once unknowingly bought and sold a mummified person, but the Mount Rushmore Amusement Park returned it as "not realistic enough."

Even in northern Peru, where the air is so dry it whines, 25 percent of hopeful mummies molder off their bones. Periodically, they poke up as skeletons at the feet of someone modern—catching time itself off guard, because they're at once present and not present, and they've traveled so long without managing to get away.

In fact, I came to realize, that very paradox had spoken to me nearly all my life—it defined a whole vein of Los Angeles desert fiction, starting with John Fante's *Ask the Dust,* whose title may be interpreted as a little less than comforting. That novel ends in the California Mojave, where the

Pacific Ocean once had its farthest northwest incursion; you can practically hear it if you stand out there alone.

Recently the *LA Times* ran a story—Tara told me—about an early human ancestor who fought a life-or-death struggle 2 million years ago "and lost." He'd entered a carnivore's den, scientists said, possibly with several helpers, planning to scrape meat from some freshly killed prey and still flee before a saber-toothed tiger caught them in the act. "Unfortunately," scientists said, "they were not always successful." Which makes me imagine the hominid's children asking, on the eve of their first hunt: "That last part, 'not always successful' . . . what does that *mean?*"

What exactly *does* it mean? Is the foreknowledge of death the beginning of wisdom? A classic *New Yorker* piece by Ian Frazier concerning bear sightings in Montana lingered memorably on the irony that hikers devoured by bears included a) doctors and b) Christian pastors—i.e., people who beforehand may have reasonably felt they had *special dispensation* as they hiked into the wild. But the bears did not understand this.

Indeed, what if God's dispensation runs the opposite way? Like the old Jewish joke about being the Chosen People ("chosen for *what?*"), any prayer for spiritual growth ought to trigger a drop-and-cover reflex. Witness Pete Fullerton, bass player of the sixties electro-folk group We Five, described as the humanitarian of the group. Leaving fame behind, he joined a ministry delivering household items to the homeless; in a short time, a skill-saw accident cut off three fingers with such "surgical precision" that the stubs formed a perfectly straight line. He struck out to experience homelessness firsthand, only to get beaten and dumped by a farmer in the deep South who drove him many miles from civilization and dared him to find his way back. When Pete made California, he was malnourished, near blind from an eye infection. He recovered and joined a house-building charity in Mexico, but fell from a roof, landing in a tree that grew out from the side of a cliff, which is where he hung while his wife sought an ambulance. They arrived at the hospital too late to save his badly broken leg, which had to be amputated. At last report, Pete and his wife were in South Carolina, ministering to a group of homeless people in a forest.

"Peter exists on a spiritual plane with which neither you nor I are familiar," one bandmate later remarked to another—suggesting, I guess, that gradual dismemberment may be a path to enlightenment reserved for God's cherished few ("God chastens whom he loves." Proverbs 3:12; "It is a fearful thing to fall into the hands of the living God." Hebrews 10:31)—and in any event, I probably didn't want to get there as badly as Pete.

Everyone in Innsbruck says the place to find Iceman merchandise is in Bolzano, a city in northern Italy a half-hour south of the glacier. If I drive there, I'll find T-shirts, lapel pins, a window display of the corpse in designer jeans. A headline in an Italian newspaper reads, "LA MUMMIA SUPERSTAR." I exit the autobahn expecting to see the sky blotted out by a giant, tethered Iceman balloon.

Instead I discover that the craze may have peaked, but there are "tours," such as one offer in the Steiermark, east of Innsbruck, to "Hike Like the Glacier Man"—basically a pair of snowshoes and a shove on the back; worse, it's two hundred miles from the find.

As a stereotype, I disappoint no one. I'm clumsy in the language; there's a leak in my parka; I arrive in a blizzard of feathers. I smile and ask to see the body. This makes me a voyeur, but I know I'm just compelled. I need to view the thing in him that I've forgotten about in myself. Mortality is fascinating—you sometimes hear it still exists. You allow that it exists, and then take a breath, and then you laugh at yourself for worrying: the coast looks pretty clear. Feeling good, I decide I'll buy an Iceman T-shirt. I decide it will make a very hip Christmas gift. So I've driven a long time around Northern Italy trying to find one, darkness falling, when I realize 1) I'm lost, 2) I've lost my passport.

Without which I can't cross back into Austria, where my hotel is. I've left the passport on the counter of a bank in Bolzano, where I had to use it to change money; only now do I remember that as I left, the bank teller, an Italian black-suited gentleman, had . . . kind of smirked. Definitely smirked. He was Death's man in Bolzano. Now the bank has closed for the weekend.

So there is no choice but to find the Austrian border, but instead I make a series of wrong turns on the nameless winding roads. Open vistas deliriously promise escape, then vanish the instant they appear. Now darkness has fallen. The temperature outside has dropped below the kind of freezing that makes your face feel tacky, and the gas gauge reads, well, around half full or half empty, depending how you see the world, ha ha. You are talking to yourself, by the way.

How resourceful is any one of us? The Iceman knew that acid from trees would tan leather. He knew how to salt animal furs to keep the hairs from falling out. He knew that the blood trail of a chamois was pink and frothy if he'd punctured the lungs and flat red if he'd gotten the heart, and he knew how long either colored trail would lead before the animal would have to have dropped. He knew how to slit the windpipe and the belly, and twist the ribs to expel the intestines, and then sit on a rock in the cold and chew the sinew until he had it conditioned into a brand new bowstring. I wasn't sure I could do any of those things, at least right away.

And if by some miracle I found the border station, would they let me through without my passport? Would they jail me as a spy? You laugh, then scold yourself for laughing, which is when a voice that you remember only in the truest moments of your life clears its throat, the voice that only ever says, *This is how we'll go*. Perhaps today, perhaps not, but this is how we're *going* to go; whether in an hour or fifty years, you will be shown a fool for imagining you could ever outrun the smirk of the Italian bank teller.

Making one final clueless turn, you see the halo of a light beyond a ridge. It is the highway. And greater lights beyond prove to be the border station, where you wail to the guard in the booth: "*Bitte helfe! Ich habe mein passport nicht!*" And he waves you through (this being the pre-9/11 world yet). You wonder if you haven't been overworried.

An extra week in Austria to get a replacement passport. It is a time of bonus-round limbo: Getting to drive 100 mph on the autobahn in blissful anonymity, only occasionally updating Tara back home, whose worry felt practically irrelevant, like when you swam underwater as a kid and your parents yelled for you to come out of the pool, their sound waves so thwarted you could pretend to yourself you didn't hear them.

My middle years would erode that smug veneer. Like repressed memories, aspects of this trip to Austria would occasionally resurface. I recalled the lamp bases made of lacquered organs, this time in the light of new articles about how Nazi scientists sold concentration-camp cadavers to universities. I wondered if the self I'd brought to Austria somehow died there, in a rapture of the Alps, and if the self who flew back to the States were his hard-luck doppelganger. (As Mark Twain wrote, "We're not sure if it was me or my identical twin who died.") My life took turns that began to hint I was paying for my escape. The marriage to Tara was spooked, almost from the outset, by traumatic pregnancy ("In pain shall you bear children"), the deaths by cancer of all but one of my living relatives, and skeletons in more closets than we knew we had; my ten years with Kriss teetered from state budget crisis to job furloughs, to home foreclosure, to the catastrophic disability of a then-teenage child. The narrative mind, my mind, can connect those particular dots back to the grace I'd used up in the Alps.

Yet I carry a beautiful, parallel scrapbook of those same years. The grown son's laugh that still surfaces, surprising even him, flagrante delicto, as if he's caught himself at hide-and-seek. The daughter's brown eyes that gaze into yours in the bizarre contentment of knowing she gives joy just being here. The youngest son, for some reason a leader, slapping his forehead as the marching Cub Scouts collide in a flag ceremony. All these new strangers trace their lives to a particular place in the Alps where I did not die. And with the years, of course, comes the grownup awareness—I didn't put it there—that nothing less than using one's time to love other people will really do, because like children playing ring-around-the-rosy, we're all here more or less cheating death.

I doubt sometimes it is a physical *there,* the place in the Alps where those roads spun around themselves, both for the Iceman and for me. If it is, I might one day show my kids. It will be a deranged nostalgia tour. *Hike like the Iceman.* We'll snap a family selfie on the spot where I felt that Shakespearean checkmate in my soul ("We owe God a death and let it go which way it will / he that dies this year is quit for the next"): Dip a toe in, then a limb, death supplying life its missing voice. Unless death is just too vast and slight a wormhole to be mapped, the falling-in as unaccountable as this morning's reprieve.

10

E Luxo So
(It's Only Luxury)

Nothing about moving from our ranch house across Encino to the new apartment village on Newcastle Avenue, which people were starting to call Little Israel, made you think that the Valley's best years were over. Hardly anyone thought nostalgically yet—even *American Graffiti* was a summer or two away. In architecture, every cut corner looked like progress, and all the new unmolded doors still looked expensive. French mansard roofs were being added to gas stations.

I was seventeen, a Valley boy. Instead of helping pack for the move, I'd spent days over the hill at Santa Monica Beach trying to tan, meet girls, prolong the instant (more like a sun-spot illusion) of hitting my best years and having my mom still have hers too.

Mom was divorced and neurotic, maybe clinically, yet

still able, at fifty-one, to laugh at herself. She was famous among my friends for starting up drug-like rounds of hysterics that caved into more laughter just when you thought she'd pulled herself together.

These were the last seconds of that: my mom pacing the new apartment, worrying where things should go, me holding past and future in some perfect Valley stasis. Until the doorbell rang, and in came the movers with the furniture that had always defined us.

First, the great white vinyl reading chair from the Nat King Cole fifties—she used to hug me in that chair and say I'd always be her baby ("He's too old for that," groaned my sister). Then, the couch: a trim thatch of brown as tailored as a diplomat. For the new decade, though, she has just had it reupholstered in rough stripes—blazing, autumnal, a seventies harvest.

Then, the eighteen-inch television on a wobbly cart. It connected us to the news team at KNBC (Tom Snyder, Kelly Lange, and Ross Porter in gleeful malfunction), whose afternoon theme song was practically a hymn to post-sixties decompression: Instead of teletype staccato and veering-ambulance brass, it traced the melody line of John Sebastian's "Darling Be Home Soon" (*Come / And talk of all the things we did today* . . .). This was a pivotal year for women filling their lungs with domestic hope. Mary Tyler Moore hammered a wobbly M to the wall of her sitcom apartment; Paul McCartney's anonymous heroine ("slipping into stockings, stepping into shoes, dipping in the pockets of her raincoat") ventured from bath to workday.

Finally, the coffee table: With its doe legs, starlet poise, and windswept marble top, it was my mom's quintessential possession, the sixties on heels. To her horror, though, it was being conveyed to the room by a single worker, surfer-style.

"Excuse me!" Mom hailed. "That's a job for two people!" She'd even phoned ahead about it.

The mover smiled, stood a little taller—plainly the woman was worrying for his health. That's when the marble nosedived from his moving blanket to the floor, snapping in two.

You could see her take the emotional blow full face. Lowering her head, she steered me to the kitchen as if for a séance.

"I can't stand it," she finally spoke.

"He wasn't trying to break the table," I said. I had to take the mover's side; I was a boy with an absent dad.

But she was too absorbed to hear—too interested, really, in finding words for what was going on deeper down. Suddenly she grasped it. "I knew I didn't like him!" The confession was childlike, utterly freeing; she even smiled a kind of dangerous smile. Her eyes went wide at the shame.

She gathered herself then, released one cleansing sigh—and the rockiness of this sigh let slip everything about how old you will feel one day too. How did a person get to be fifty? When, in the course of staying young at heart, would everything start to seem a little less funny than sad?

"Come home, America!" George McGovern wailed that summer at the Democratic National Convention.

For me and my girlfriend Kim, lounging by the pool at the Newcastle Manor Apartments, summer was a dream. That we thought getting drunk a perfectly valid nightly entertainment troubled my mother but also impressed her. Part of Mom's vestigial Jewishness was that she couldn't help loving anyone who made me happy even temporarily; it meant I'd escaped a million worse fates.

Kim was ten pounds too heavy in white cutoffs, a look my more experienced friends called just right but with which I found fault. Her Jungle Gardenia perfume made the night air redundant.

She invented her own words ("squozen orange juice") and once wore a false mustache to help me pretend I was drinking with the guys. Your first girlfriend is a free gift from God.

When my mom was at work, we staggered indoors from baking at the pool—it was like we'd been working at some erotic foundry—stripped off our wet bathing suits and had sex on the carpet. At that age I had no idea how scandalously young her skin would seem looking back, those melted-sundae tan lines. Beneath me Kim vibrated but never climaxed, a fact that unmanned me to my soul. But she insisted she was happy. Afterward we enacted Mellow Time: I shared my records and my comic collection, and we timed things so we were sipping coffee when Mom got home with dinner.

Whatever the sin tax is on a luxury apartment, in short, it was my mother who paid it. Yet she wasn't sad or resentful about her life. Even if she felt some drop-off from her old milieu as a doctor's wife and a conductor of surveys at Hollywood's Preview House, something in her longed for the middle of the herd. The men she dated post-divorce were a fence builder with scabby knuckles, a big-rig driver who ironed his jeans, and a cardsharp heart patient who went by "Fast Eddie." The last spent one visit to our home drunk and sobbing that he didn't deserve our company because we were such decent people: sensitive, educated, Jewish.

When the cardsharp disappeared, Mom bought a red velour pantsuit at Montgomery Ward's and started hitting the Ventura Club, a phase that ended when a guy with flashy rings propositioned her: "I've never made it with a blonde before." It was proof of her Iowa upbringing that the worst retort she could muster was to call him a "yokel"; it was the mark of her Valleyness that she hurried home to tell the story to her children.

That began her boyfriend-less years. She stopped swimming too, no longer able to stand the red gooseflesh of her chest and neck in a bathing suit. The crepe-paper thighs.

"Just swim, Mom. No one cares."

"You don't *understand!*" she says, with those rocks in her lungs, the sigh that always made her sound babyish and elderly at once.

The days glided by in this manner. Kim and I were repeat customers at Planned Parenthood. But we were adored.

Everyone in this Kesselgarden welcomed everyone else, lost souls on chaise lounges, rich and poor together. They had so little in common besides ethnicity you could wonder if they'd been moved there for a genocidal purpose.

I met the wiry owner of a Pacoima department store (it meant an instant stockroom job for me) who lounged at the pool the way executives do: almost prettily. The stockroom workers feared him deeply, but at Newcastle he was fine with being just a renter.

There was a woman barely thirty whom I thought of inexplicably as a cancer victim, that sense of bad makeup, with her nose a shade lighter than her face. She held herself back from the pool in a way that implied she was always on her period, and her figure looked fine from up front, but slack from the side. I noticed all this because she was so close to attractive. It drove me crazy trying to pinpoint what wasn't sexy about her. She was friendly to me, or possibly rooting for me ("If I were ten years younger, boy—watch out!"), which meant my mom had been winning her over to my worrisome cause. But in some way she struck me as what was left of a body when you robbed it of all a family's blessings. She was like McCartney's office girl, only without the knack of making her loneliness look like the world's loss instead of her own.

But there were happier residents. There was the high-school student, Bill, and his girlfriend, Charla, whose baby skin he praised so generously ("Look! Look at that complexion!"), one arm curled around her, you felt like he couldn't really be her boyfriend. *Why wasn't he scared of building her up?* She looked so bored atop this unearned pedestal, but what confused me most was Bill. He had the serene self-esteem of a whole different kind of Jew, some royal kind that my mother and I were too tone-deaf somehow to be.

I found my own level. I smoked dope with a fifteen-year-old Eurasian girl who taunted her mother for pidgin English. She lit up with me in the sauna room, toking in a penguin squat, her eyes closed for minutes at a time. She seemed generally intent on punishing her mother for being the parent who stayed.

The building's other Asian, a housewife in a white bikini, invited me inside just once to get high—the kind of proposition the whole decade seemed to keep tossing up like a koan. My friend Scott stood guard outside the door while Tricia sat yoga-style on her carpet, ferns everywhere, like some raga-inflected poster, extending the reefer. Sand-white lipstick, turquoise necklace, brick brown skin, the whole palette of 1970s Eden.

I made friends with the building's Jewish cop, which I felt was an odd, almost cross-dressing job for a Jew to have, but I couldn't explain why. Inevitably, he was suing the police force for harassment. He loaned me his diary, which seemed obsessed with a particular picture postcard that some coworkers stole from above his desk. *Why won't they give me back my postcard?* each day's entry began. Naturally I wanted to know what the postcard depicted—but it seemed too personal a thing to ask about, and I might prove myself a pervert if I assumed. With a hateful smirk, he told me about a much scummier cop who used his badge to get freebies at massage parlors—the implication seemed to be that if I could only see what was pictured on my friend's postcard, I would have known what the world and all its rotten policemen were too coarse to appreciate.

Soon, in fact, my mom started working at a porn shipping warehouse in Reseda. For a woman who flipped through *Playboy* in search of new hairstyles, this wasn't a monumental departure, but it was a next degree of separation from her market-research friends in Hollywood. When the warehouse was short-handed, I pitched in, and for all the titillation in the air we might have been shipping geriatric supplies, possibly to the same national network of shut-ins. Knowing a stranger's secrets, especially hand printed on mail-order forms, released a hormone of sacred responsibility: You wanted every hand that wrote those letters to feel unjudged. I wasn't sure if my mom looked up or down at this community, but she was happy. There was that solid ground of self-acceptance that always is the unexpected blessing of landing a little lower than you've aimed in life.

At the same time, some bridge back to the sixties was being demolished. Moonlighting in market research, Mom recruited me for a consumer focus group on underground rock music; we were about as hip as Old World matchmakers in not foreseeing the contradictions of that concept.

The band was Pablo Cruise. From my armrest, I dialed up hopeful tens at the onset of each Blazing Guitar Riff—

only to scurry back to zero when it was plain there would be no real solo. The decade of canned improvisation was upon us.

Mom and I deplored this sacrilege together. But feeling superior to your times is never a joke that ends well.

Not that I could afford to worry for her sake; I had my own escape to launch. I had to become popular, perfect, maybe famous. It was every Jew for himself. Recovering from heartbreak, on New Year's Day I decided to quit smoking and get in shape at the same time; I'd left Kim only to be rejected by one of those black-haired girls from Encino Hills who always dismissed you in the end because she had a successful dad who adored her and she had been to Erhard Seminars Training at seventeen, which meant she was just complicated enough to find your sadness fascinating, until something fascinated her more.

To dwell deeply on being rejected would have killed me, so like some underage soldier whose whole platoon just got blown up, I sprang into self-help. At every bowl-game timeout I dropped for fifty pushups. I was going to be as hard-bodied and untouchable as the San Gabriel Mountains.

Walking to the fridge around sundown, however, I felt a twinge, ghostly but precise, in my groin, the kind of signal that says Not One Step More. I froze, and like a prank the pain left. Yet things were not right. It was as if my name had been called, as if the safety of the past was all a prologue. There came a second, unmistakably larger, pain.

This pattern would repeat itself in my body for the next six months.

I had rented a place in Sherman Oaks, a few miles east of my mom, which felt either too far or too close for comfort. The Santa Ana winds on New Year's Day stripped the atmosphere like gauze from a wound, and life seemed thrilling but also desperate, a spacewalk—without nets, without cigarettes, without Mom. And yet simultaneously with her: surviving on the fumes of her generation's hopes. At some point that week I announced to a friend and his fiancée that I would never have children: The world was too harsh for innocent life. I'm not absolutely certain I meant business, but I found it safer to call the world a trickster than to trust it like a sheltered child myself.

With my new affliction, of course, I was a sidelined Casanova. During my chastity, Playboy pinups became talismanically powerful, but stroking to them hurt so bad I stopped.

Lab tests, more lab tests, and finally a diagnostic procedure under general anesthesia—in the hazy pain-pill aftermath of which, suddenly, all was grooviness and new beginnings. The ache in my groin had left, or I stopped caring. I glided around poolside at my mom's. Ordered not to swim, I swam anyway. That ended my bout with chronic prostatitis.

But the real breakthrough came a week before the procedure. She called to say she'd had a dream. In it, I was happy, tan, and open-shirted, with an abalone shell necklace, with the ocean behind me receiving the setting sun like the first mai tai of summer. She believed this vision was a sign—although in truth, its loveliness was so transient, so physical, it contained its own cellular dread: You could worry it was just a fool's reprieve. But you could also kick that worry ahead. Things were going to be OK, Mom insisted, almost with her famous giggle, and my body more or less cooperated. She was as philosophically weaponless against worry as I was—and just as surprised when illness passed. So she did faith healings now, too.

But how many healings did she have left? What I didn't want to face was that her sixties divorcée mentality was becoming a turned page. In her Depression-era soul, there had always lived a worrier. But for one unique span of years, a spirit of play more or less ravished her. Like lots of San Fernando Valley dwellers in the sixties, she'd learned to *wear life loosely*.

She'd found hobbies, almost all of which I've tried to wring magic from in my own middle life: country music, horse-race betting, guitar lessons, a pool table with house rules for the short-armed room. She smoked in the dark, which made even dedicated worry look romantic. She had her dreams of glamour, but she wasn't so vain as to think she knew best what the cosmic plan was. In the Valley, where movie stars came to stop living like stars, or to hide their perversions from the light, a separate wave of guilt-fleeing Americans went white trash. They threw Pop-Tarts at the kids for breakfast or woke us for midnight Yahtzee. What kid could resist a giggling parent?

Until she'd sold our house, for $60,000 on the eve of the real-estate boom. And we moved to Newcastle Avenue on land that was once Adohr Farms, beside what had once been RKO studios, on the former set of Bedford Falls, from *It's a Wonderful Life—that* Valley.

Of all my Encino friends growing up, only Steve D. wasn't Jewish. I'm not really sure why so many Jews, because no Jewish families I knew came to the Valley looking for Jewish life. Steve was a natural athlete, and he had his way with girls, maybe because gentiles like him had no ethnic demon to overcome, or maybe because his parents wouldn't mind if he just sold auto parts with his dad.

But when the Jewish girl he fell for in high school picked Steve M. instead—a Jewish kid whose dad my mom knew from college in Chicago—D. was blindsided. M. had charisma, but D.'s was so much more telegenic you wondered if tribal bigotries explained his being snubbed. I drank with D. till my thirties, and the last time I saw him, when we were both forty-something, he still talked about losing this girl who should have been his.

The royalty at my high school consisted of Latinos with Anglicized first names alongside Encino Hills girls with hip-hugger jeans and orthodontia. The girls were free about sex but, unlike their blonde Van Nuys counterparts, only if the boyfriend had a future. Jewish girls did the seventies with parents on board.

As for Jewish guys, they had more of a long-shot air (*"Aleph, Bet, Gimmel, Dalid, we got a team that's really solid,"* ran the school cheer), but the ones from the hills had new feathered haircuts and really nice cars, and they were starting to rise. This put me on the fringe of either an envied minority or an ironic majority—Jews assimilating with Gentiles who were being left behind by Jews.

My mom's Jewishness was even fringier. She was proud of Jews for making it big ("God helps those who help themselves") and for focusing on healing the world (*Tikkun olam*), but she was a pariah in other ways. Our first temple, Valley Beth Shalom, took good liberal stands on busing and Prop. 187 (its rabbi preached against supernaturalism and was Hollywood enough to help writers for *The Simpsons* develop Krusty the Clown)—but when their audit of my mom's finances to set membership dues turned inquisitional, she fled to Temple Judea, near Newcastle, almost as rich but less toney. There were fewer sunglasses on high holidays, more sloppy kisses on the cheeks of kids like me.

A gulf had begun to widen. The same year we moved to Newcastle, B'nai B'rith of Encino began distributing Passover boxes to elderly Jews in the flatlands. By 1995, they were loading 3 million pounds of necessities onto trucks behind Gelson's on Hayvenhurst—so iconic a grocer to the hill people that it became the punch line of a joke. (An old man thinks his moaning wife is finally, finally responding to his lovemaking, until she completes her sentence: "Ohhhh-hhhhhhhh you would not have BELIEVED the lines at Gelson's.")

Gradually the Kesselgarden got less cohesive, more expensive. There were condo conversions. Residents peeked through their curtains at young arrivals from the Midwest or the East Coast who figured they'd found Hollywood with easier traffic. Soon, when Newcastle Avenue made news, it was the police-show kind of news. A twenty-nine-year-old woman strangled her sixty-eight-year-old boyfriend with a strap from his overalls, because he wouldn't abide her female lover. A male tenant got shot in the face by a female friend who told police they were acting out scenes from *Miami Vice*. Several buildings were accused of hiding vacancies from black renters, prompting tremulous denials in the *LA Times*. ("I have preached ever since I can remember," pleaded one manager, "that everyone's blood is red.")

In 2002, a Newcastle tenant named David Cohen disconnected a gas line for repair and lit a cigarette, causing an explosion that left 300 homeless and collapsed the recreation room. The swimming pool water was "an oily black," reported the *Daily News*. Refugees searching for units in the neighborhood found that most rents were now beyond their range. Some moved a block west to Zelzah, where two buildings within the next year caught fire, one of them requiring thirteen engine companies to control. "These streets are bad luck," said one tenant to reporters.

I followed all this with half a heart. When Jews of my generation react to ethnic tragedy, there's often this campy, inverse pride—the same sort of grotesque self-inoculation that made captured journalist Daniel Pearl's last words ("I'm a Jewish American from Encino, California") available as an Mp3 ringtone.

It's funny about my people. If we're not total hostages of creative risk—Bob Dylan, Leonard Cohen, Andy Kauffman, or Paul Simon—we're its most cuddly genius hacks: Barry Manilow, Neil Diamond, Barbra Streisand. We can't deal with the opposite type of Jew within ourselves. J. D. Salinger was the second type before he became the first. If Norman Mailer was ever the second, it happened long before he chose his alter ego. Producer Rick Rubin started in rap, but, perhaps feeling pangs of *mamaloshen,* he styled himself a gangsta rabbi and rehabilitated Neil Diamond.

How the Valley altered the equation, though, in showing the nation exactly how to stylize postwar safety, was to make every American teen an imitation Valley girl and every popular Valley artist an honorary Jew. The Jacksons and Bobby Sherman (both of whom attended my high school) and Andrew Gold (who did not) all seem like pathological and loyal Jewish sons; their accidental genius is to reconcile the hemispheres of the American Jewish mind—integrity and pile carpet, prophecy and flesh.

You don't have to be Jewish to be caught in this pathology. For instance, I don't know how much to make of drummer Jim Gordon (gentile, Grant High). He played with Delaney & Bonnie at the Peppermint Twist on Ventura, a portal halfway to Hollywood, joined Derek and the Dominoes, cowrote Eric Clapton's "Layla," the almost naive piano progression that's virtually too pure for the song, lingering on that diminished chord and then resolving it over and over, as if to say, "Oooooh . . . *sorrow,*" which made it no less perfect. All the smooth, Eagles-inflected sounds of the Newcastle pool seemed implicit in Gordon's adventure. He was our scout to the scary outer world, playing Vegas while garaging his white Mercedes down the block.

As the eighties dawned, Gordon went mad. In auditory

hallucinations, he heard his mother commanding him to starve. To silence the voices, he killed her in 1983 and landed in Atascadero State Prison, where he remains, medicated and dreaming in interviews that he'll reunite with Clapton. According to the *Philadelphia Inquirer,* Gordon's hideout during the worst throes of schizophrenia was Sportsman's Lodge on Ventura, scene of wishing-well bridges, Bing Crosby cardigans, and my Bar Mitzvah party—*that* Valley. By the time he arrived, of course, the hotel was a campy ghost, the place where my generation's rock royalty goofed, seventies-style, on being stately gluttons with ruffled shirts: heirs and heiresses.

A director of religious education named Natalie Smolens had been at my old temple since forever, so two summers ago I went to interview her. I was going through the end of my ten-year marriage to Kriss, and my beloved grown son, along for the ride to Tarzana, brought enough psychiatric difficulty of his own—complete with stupefying medication—that waiting in a parked car for me to finish a two-hour interview was, tragically, not a challenge.

We cruised my old neighborhood first. The ranch house, which my mom sold for $60,000 in 1972, is today a high-walled fortress. Glen Ballard, the Grammy-winning producer who recorded Alanis Morissette's *Jagged Little Pill,* sold it for $1.5 million in 2006. The surrounding homes look exactly like they used to, but indefinably more expensive—until you realize it's not the houses, it's the cars.

On Ventura, split-level courtyard malls with palm trees

have replaced gas stations and steak houses. Toward Tarzana, things look more ethnic: same old everything but gone Iranian. The All American Newsstand. The Glatt Kosher Market.

What hasn't changed is the sweet forsaken Valley ease. The air tastes like sand. Under the harsh sun, the men look like highbrow disappointments, and the long perspectives make a woman out walking look parentless. I feel like she could need me.

To get to Natalie Smolens, I have to pass a day care where both the kids and the moms look more Mediterranean than they used to; there's construction all around for a new $26 million synagogue, and the old gravel parking lot features a guard in a booth. I tell myself that every odyssey turns strangest near the point of return. The more vagabond you feel, the more perfectly you've raised your prayer for home. This is so fucking Jewish of me.

Smolens is built strong at seventy-six, with a crisp solid blouse untucked and plenty of pearls and rings, and I know this style: It's how my oldest sister dressed in the business world, ritz on a budget. Like most temple Jews I've known, she takes religion piecemeal while overflowing with humanism, and I always wonder if the reason they're so stable is that God has left them alone. She offers a bottle of water from the mini fridge, and before I can switch on the recorder, I'm kind of confessing: This is where my mom's brief Valley heyday ended.

But Smolens doesn't understand at first—she thinks I'm disparaging the neighborhood. "Why do you say brief?" she asks vigorously. "This is news to me. I'd like you, when you leave here, to drive up Reseda Boulevard heading south, and you tell me what your impression is. It's by far not a slum! And the rentals are not cheap!"

Well, I say, what about the fires, the condo conversions, how there used to be such a mix of rich and poor you couldn't tell one from the other? Smolens agrees. In fact, she says, she doesn't know anyone on Newcastle anymore, nothing that's the same, except the newsstand.

That newsstand! "How does it survive?" I ask.

"It's mostly porn—I suppose that's what keeps it alive," she says, and now we've found our subject. I mention my mom's old job, but Smolens can do better. "We have a dad in the business—in fact, a couple of dads. We had a very active family, since divorced. One of the moms in our school—I am *told*. I'm better off not knowing. Firsthand, I had one young couple years ago: Her father started the business, and her husband joined him."

"But doesn't the temple feel a conflict with any of this?"

Smolens frowns. "You're saying, what—that morally they should not have been accepted?"

"I just mean, how do they reconcile making porn with religion?"

"I don't know. Maybe they have to do enough good deeds, to—I don't *know!*" she says, with my mom's bewildered pout. "It's the fear of annihilation that connects us as Jews," she says. She's surprised she has to tell me.

As I'm leaving, we bond about parenting. I beg an extra bottled water for my son, and Smolens knows how I'm feeling, and worse: Her own son died at sixteen of leukemia. "Is there anything worse than watching your child in pain?"

"I always thought I'd get a pass," I tell her.

"Look," she says, taking a chance. "Do you get for yourself a support system? Because you're going through hell. You need to take care of you first. Get yourself somebody to talk to. I remember when my son was suffering—I kind of lost sometimes my logic. He would be forty now."

I nod.

"You have to find the good. I know it sounds stupid." All at once it hits her. "Oh, my Lord. I do know someone! On Newcastle!" Smolens heads to her desk phone. "My girlfriend's son is married to a woman whose parents live— right there! They're probably in their eighties now, and they still walk every day up Newcastle to the corner, holding hands."

Obviously this is a couple I should interview. Smolens punches in a number.

"Joey? It's Natalie Smolens. Your grandmother's friend. How are you? Joey, do you have the number of your mom's parents on Newcastle Avenue?"

A pause. A long pause—the news is bad, and I watch it land.

"Oh. I didn't know. I'm so sorry, honey. Beverly never said a word."

Toward the end of the seventies, my mom started bringing home the works of one of those LeRoy Neiman–type painters with a matadorial style. I wasn't coming over so often, but when I did, it looked to me like she was suffering from a crisis in taste. We connected over Beatles albums, but now she liked the saccharine ones, the ballad-heavy anthologies that met her generation more than halfway. When I played piano, she'd have me plod through the chords of George Harrison's "Something," and she'd sit next to me adding moony refrains. I'd sing, "I don't want to leave her now," and she'd chime, emphysemically, "Oh, no."

I did want to leave her, sort of. I wanted to escape the horror-show loneliness of a Valley stripped to its essence of middle-American hope. The Valley that invested in burial plots and CD accounts was too close to the shadow of death. It was where my mother gave up swimming. It was where we hung Peanuts wall plaques, monuments to melancholia and invisible parents and encroaching shadows. In so many ways, the Valley's dark twin was winning out: assembly-line Pintos, mini-malls, the end of cruise night on Van Nuys Boulevard.

Teaching herself proofreading marks from *Webster's,* Mom strained her eyes correcting airplane specs and then civic history books, lunching on a single red apple to save money for her kids, another sure sign of the end. But I never had the guts to refuse her aid if my wallet was empty. The history books were subsidized by local merchants who paid for their own write-ups, and the offices felt invaded by corporate looky-loos; not even publishing could harbor oddballs anymore.

So in 1980, I made my escape to the just-launched *LA Weekly* in Hollywood as a substitute proofreader, dressed like a job-seeker from guidance class, and in my rearview mirror the Valley became a farm field, my Iowa: a big-sky backdrop to the frigid contrails of aerospace.

She had been priced out of Newcastle Manor by then. She found a Van Nuys condo with plastic fake-wood ceiling beams that she was too nearsighted to question until the adhesive came loose at one end. The neighborhood was multiethnic, not remotely Jewish, but comfortable in its alienated way, and from that time forward she seemed to curl herself up in housebound pleasures (pound cake, Alex Trebek) until she died of emphysema, which is no way to go. In the end, those rocky sighs became constant: all out-breaths, like her whole mission was to calm herself down to say goodbye. And she captured that last unfairness with a child's heart too, complaining, "I don't know how to die!" until she did.

I live in Long Beach, forty years after the summer Mom and I moved to Little Israel. I'm blessed with a couple of young kids sword-fighting on the lawn and my grown son behind earbuds in his room, and somehow I'm the go-to for all of them—because, as a friend of mine likes to say, God has my paperwork mixed up with somebody strong.

A few things on our weekly itinerary remind me of my mom's Valley: the Kaiser Mental Health Center in Norwalk (the way a suburban hospital throws a shadow over the tracts and the backyard pools). The checker at our neighborhood Trader Joe's—blonde, raspy, and sunburned, like every Valley dreamer used to be but mostly meth heads are now. She practically adopts me for having a struggling loved one in tow, and she reaches out to him the only way she knows, by lovingly cussing at him to smile.

Most things, though, seem utterly alien. The rooms of my single-dad apartment staring back like I've landed from a bender. Some days, Long Beach feels like a penal asteroid.

I walk to Walgreens to get *E-Z Crosswords* (a hopeless homage to Mom's swamp-cooler years) and cheap colored pencils for my kids, and absolutely nothing is the same about buying colored pencils today, except that by some mistake the twenty-first century still sells colored pencils.

I realize that my summers by the pool got used up young, and like Kim, they spoiled me for the world. My mom's moment in history, like the San Fernando Valley's, like the California Dream's, ended just when a lot of Americans thought they'd caught a break. You can find statistical corroboration everywhere for what your eyes and ears know to be true: that around 1972, the U.S. turned from one of the most egalitarian societies on Earth to one of the least, that in retrospect the luxury apartments on Newcastle were just a holding cell before the crumbling condos with the fake beam ceilings. The later Valley immigrants have it right: work three low-wage jobs, find love and freedom in struggle by being all in. It's just not a formulation that the balcony apartments were built for.

Mom would never have called the National Association for Mental Illness for a family support group.

She never would have felt like God was hiding, because she wasn't seeking. Fun surprised her, delighted her—it was her weakness and her strength.

I will wean my son from all his stupid medications. I'll envision him happy and tan, the way my mom did me when I had prostatitis. Everything will prove psychosomatic.

I buy Yahtzee.

When I was choosing music for my mother's funeral in 1997, the weirdest part was how her favorite album from the good days (*Jazz Samba,* by Stan Getz and Charlie Byrd) sounded like it was composed for the occasion—specifically composed to haunt some future room with the memory of how breezy life could be.

The rhythm section, made of soft bass and snare brushes, is the reassuring tone of a darkened house, of bare feet on carpet as heard from a child's bedroom like mine. Getz's reeds, too, are deftly adult, rueful, musing, retiring yet tossed off, like a French girl shrugging her coat. For me, it's the precise image of the coffee table that broke. It's the exact glide of a woman at the end of a day in 1972.

Like everyone else, I have this yen to heal the world, tinged by my mom's slightly too childish complaint—a Jewish thing: *Tikkun olam.*

At the St. Luke's shower-and-meals program on Saturdays, I pray with the homeless, and plenty of them give more comfort than they take. The tormented ones are earning crowns in heaven.

Some nights, I can't go to sleep without looking at Internet porn.

I discover my son is going to be a dad. Rub some years on all of this. Learn to trust time.

Alan Rifkin

A pickup truck tours by, booming some violent song.

What the hell did we do with that big white chair from the Valley? Where my sister complained, "He's too old for that," and my mom said, "He'll never be too old for that."

1 1

Writing in the Dust

I can still picture, if only barely, Evelyn Waugh arriving in Los Angeles back when not everything here had been named yet, and seeing the double meanings laid so bare—oasis and dust, paradise and exile—that he finished a novel in ten weeks (*The Loved One,* his sendup of an immortality-crazed mortuary) after it had taken him three years to write the one before.

Of course, the famous ironies of the Southern California landscape have gotten pretty gentrified since then. They've been coming true and getting commonplace at the same time—growing up.

It happened fast, because when I was growing up here and wanted to write, I could still detect at least the tail wind of Waugh's delirium—that hallucinatory, step-outside-time awareness of standing on our own graves. And I know this gets hazy. But in the California that I'm remembering, mostly Valley in my case, mostly seventies and eighties, I could tan and pretend there would never be cancers, or at least write about people who did. ("The goddess of the coast and the germ of a bag lady," as I once described a character.) I could make up histories out of place names, before the last figments vanished from the highway. I could wager everything on madness, like Pascal, because madness might be a latter-day prophecy. Or some kind of R. D. Laing exercise in going sane. There were outside rumors, of course, that madness wasn't really sane at all. But I wasn't sure of this yet in Los Angeles.

We were going to be ageless, find the Garden, reinvent brotherhood (or show where it had been lost).

At the same time I knew, like Waugh, that we were dreaming. And, as I was starting to realize, this reality disorder had been the starting point, the given, for an entire generation of local novelists. "In Los Angeles, it is always the first generation," the poet Kate Braverman once said— a group too quiet, too neglected, to consider itself a literary movement, except maybe in its secret fantasies. But that is where some neglect can begin to pay off.

The fact is, LA has always been pulling a certain type of writer away from realistic fiction toward something more permeable that no one ever bothered to name. Any aficionado can recite a short list of hallucinatory LA visions from the twentieth century, by people like Nathanael West and John Fante and Joan Didion and Carolyn See. They were a recurring dream that shook the bed once or twice each generation, like little earthquakes. Not that the writers themselves got too vocal about the subject, except in private.

It could just seem so personal. The gorgeous estrangement. The flakiness, the longing. The possibly delusional proposition that the conflicts most central to the human condition—truth and illusion, spirit and flesh, heaven and earth, race and community—were reaching endgame mainly in Los Angeles.

In 2005, at the *Los Angeles Times* Festival of Books, I met Francesca Lia Block, whose dozen-plus metamorphic novels since the mid-1980s, including the popular Weetzie Bat oeuvre, had been turning Hollywood's fallen angels into something like pagan myth. An hour's worth of fans had lined up for her autograph, but unless she was lying, the highlight of her day was getting asked questions about the making of an LA fabulist—in her case, a childhood steeped in Greek mythology and Melrose Avenue. She talked about how orphaned she'd felt when punk monogamists John Doe and Exene split up, and how she didn't break through to her own brand of hallucinogenic fairy tale (I think her novels are Young Adult; they're also seriously horny) until she'd gone away to Berkeley, and her father was dying, and she yearned for a Hollywood lullaby. There seemed something almost stubbornly vulnerable about the proposition she'd kept staking her career on. ("How can I tell you this without sounding too crazy, too West Coast?" she told the *New York Times*. "I believe life is infused with magic.") Yet all her success had streamed from this quintessential LA foolishness: writing as if no young generation elsewhere had really been young.

Then there's Steve Erickson, whom even those who love

him struggle to get, but I get him, because he keeps writing the serial dreams of my Valley childhood: moon bridges, sand dunes, secret portals to Forever. Not that he trusted these visions right away. First he had to write five unpublished novels. "The whole activity," he told me once, "in the eyes of people I knew, and maybe even my own, began to seem a little insane"—a word that in Erickson's mouth has the hiss of someone spotting a nemesis across the room. He finally began *Days Between Stations* when he felt "there was nothing to lose, and therefore I could allow myself to bury LA under a sandstorm."

It's a literature that can seem like tag-team dreaming. After Didion's freeway dissociation in *Play It as It Lays* came Carolyn See's post-apocalyptic *Golden Days.* Then Block gave us the Weetzie Bat series, about a teenager whose offspring—by two fathers, if anyone's counting—is named Cherokee: "a girl love-warrior who would grow up to wear feathers and run swift and silent through the LA canyons."

"Can we get past plot, already?" asks novelist Martha Sherrill, an LA native half-seriously complaining about her new East Coast–writer crowd. She herself invented a starlet for an *Esquire* cover story—a magical-realist hoax—and then turned it into the novel *My Last Movie Star.*

Only in Los Angeles would so many novels, from West's *The Day of the Locust* to Robert Stone's *Dog Soldiers,* begin in realism and veer to something like biblical extra innings.[1]

---

1. "Fuckin' L.A., man," says Stone's Nietzschean protagonist, "go out for a Sunday spin, you're a short hair from the dawn of creation."

Indeed, when I moved south to be a family man in Long Beach, I started going to church—relieved to stop reinventing the language of religion from the desert floor up. But I knew I'd lost something, too. I wanted to be unmoored again—I wanted to give up God to resume the quest for Him. Like Block when she was exiled to Berkeley, I started a novella that grew out of LA memories—of bottle glass, tile chips, sagebrush in the hard mud of Malibu. After that came a novel I'm forever trying to finish, which arrived as the vision of a fasting man's pantry in 1940s Sherman Oaks. Carolyn See, riffing on what she says is a notion from Orthodox Judaism—and giving it a sort of Caltrans spin— told me once that she loosely believes Los Angeles to be one of the "twelve exits to heaven." I must have been thinking that, too. What I wanted was for my protagonist's pantry to have all these brand names that may never have existed, because if I could have named them, the secret off-ramp would have closed, the pantry would merely have been real. And then I couldn't have written.

All fiction is at some level dreamy, or it wouldn't be fiction. And novels from the bizarro LA may not be the most masterful fiction in the world. But they're the only American fiction that always looks beyond life's veil—to me the only fiction that's always worth reading.

Sometimes when I go to bookstores—where the first thing apparent is that our culture writes much too much and needs to shut up, needs some fundamentalist-futurist Ministry of Thought to cut us back to two or three nice books a year—I try works by Richard Russo or Vikram Seth or Annie Dillard, skilled outsiders, realists. The characters and manners are rendered deftly, the circle of life full and complete. But that's the problem. For all their storytelling, they only corroborate the veil of the senses. You feel reassured by them, or you should, but five minutes later, you smell a rat. Because who says the circle of life should be trusted?

And if you've surrendered, somewhere in the course of an LA childhood, to distrusting what the rest of the country deems familiar, the distrust becomes what's familiar, the local strangeness reassuring.

So I read Joy Nicholson's *The Road to Esmeralda,* in which an LA writer, haunted by his chicken-hawk dad from Yucca Valley, flees with his girlfriend into Mexican doom, post-9/11. While not actually bending the laws of physics—delirium in the jungle is so real it's practically ordinary—this book is prophetic: It chases the vanishing LA dream straight out of LA, finding no corner of the world unspoiled, no innocence left.

Or I read Erickson's *Our Ecstatic Days,* in which the portal to history, conscience, and maternal memory is a black LA lake that fills the lower floors of the Hotel of the Thirteen Losses, whose hallways are sailed by a doctor learning to specialize in buildings that are dying of grief.[2]

---

2. When a mom dives into the vortex to recover her lost son, her voice becomes a river of type that bisects each of the next 231 pages, then rejoins the text when she's back, sucking air—a typographical stunt so exacting that, rather than try to replicate it, Simon & Schuster opted to publish a jpeg of the author's original manuscript.

If you include writers with one foot in fantasy/sci-fi—if your LA vision leans toward time travelers and mermen with vestigial gills—the list becomes a catalog: Octavia Butler, Kem Nunn, James Blaylock, Scott Bradfield, Tim Powers, Kim Stanley Robinson, and all the descendants of Philip K. Dick.

Sometimes this LA literature jumps the ropes of literature itself. The urban theorist Norman Klein, who in another metropolis might set off a manhunt with nets, leads "anti-tours" of the city's "erasures" (lost pasts) and "social imaginaries"—things like trucked-in Victorian homes that create a "collective memory of an event or place that never occurred but is built anyway."

Even a *New York Times* op-ed by humorist Bruce Wagner—whose screenplays and novels of decadent Hollywood have drawn comparisons to both Charles Dickens and William Burroughs—began with mayoral politics and wound up staring at blackened hills:

> . . . I am trying to remember who Antonio Villaraigosa is—I keep giving him the name "Vargas" in my mind, like the illustrator who used to do those pin-up paintings for Playboy, Alberto Vargas—but now I am remembering that he's the new mayor, I either dreamed that or it's true, and all any of us can do is hope that he will do something terrible or scandalous or flat-out crazy so we may always remember who he is and not think we are seeing his picture in a group photo in "The Shining" or starting to read about him in a newspaper that no

longer exists and is crumbling in our hands before we can even finish.

The miracle being, perhaps, that an editor at the *New York Times* understood the sensibility behind those lines. Or pretended to, in the spirit of bicoastalism. Or caught on that a story was breaking out West that might not be understood until it was too late in the Eastern news day to report it. There's about that much connection left between Los Angeles and the commercially attentive outer world: They get that we're closer than they are to the vortex.

That isn't to say that visionary writing never happens back East. You hear sometimes of people in New York City who've dreamed. Colson Whitehead's *The Intuitionist* created a world of elevator maintenance that merged into the metaphysics of race and ascendance. Bernard Malamud concocted a talking Jewbird, and Paul Auster wrote about a vaudevillian runaway learning to levitate. I also think I see a parallel in Ben Katchor's "Julius Knipl, Real Estate Photographer" cartoons: the dream-time back alleys, the almost plausible wholesale signage (Mortal Coil Mattresses), the vaguely theosophical insomnia clubs, with marathon lectures and fluorescent lights up bright.

But the origin of those dreams always turns out to be some fixed point in the definable past: the industrial age, the melting pot, the gothic South.[3] Those writers don't actually step outside time. They don't gaze into eternity for a living—although the Mojave wind may shift in their direction from time to time. "But what is the meaning of this?" John Cheever asked in his diary, freaking out while writing "The Swimmer" (a 1964 short story that some MR fans claim as magical realist). "One does not grow old in the space of an afternoon. Oh, well, kick it around."

What's unique here is as near as Salvador Plascencia's mythic lettuce pickers in El Monte, and Ry Cooder's aural ghosts of Chávez Ravine. Playwright Jose Rivera, in *Cloud Tectonics,* posited a Mexican hitchhiker who'd been pregnant for two years. "The stories my grandparents told me," explains Plascencia, "were like Steinbeck, but with magic and witches."

Whether Latino or not, LA's literary visions always struck me as incestuously unique—a pidgin of images that simply couldn't have been composed anyplace else. Joy Nicholson says she hosted foreign guests at her Silver Lake apartment, first-time visitors who marveled from the picture window: "It's so ugly! It's so beautiful!" (They also refused bus directions to the Getty Museum—"We'll just walk"—a visual that could inspire a jungle novel all its own.) Ugly beauty is why LA's fabulist literature, even if better than the rest of the country's, will never *be* the country's, unless LA's strangeness fades out first. Here, when

---

3. "The only [other] place I can imagine it happening in this country is in the South," says Erickson. "Because in a way you could argue that the novels of Faulkner provided a basis for the fabulism that came out of South America. That whole idea of a mythical county, with mythical people. The stories aren't fabulist, but there's certainly enough psychosis in them to push them into the realm of the surreal. . . . I just think that cities like New York or Chicago are too impenetrable to allow for the kind of breakdown that makes for fabulism. There's something about the porousness of L.A.'s identity."

Francesca Lia Block confronts oleanders, they "look like cigarette cherries," and an anorexic character has "hip bones like part of an animal skull." Here, Kate Braverman's junkies accuse the surf with their tears, and the waves grow spines. Beauty and barrenness are inseparable, as every Angeleno instinctively knows them to be. Nicholson describes in an e-mail how she used to walk into the desert after dark, daring death:

> *I'd heard there were bikers and killers and freaks there, and I wondered if they would find me, and if I might come to a bad end with them . . . I just wanted to know if I would snap out of my numbness. . . . (Obviously I wanted my father to rescue me—so I put myself in the "driest, worst desert" again and again—to see if he would come through. I guess maybe I was waiting for an Oasis to come to me.)*

For me, it was always man-made lakes—starting with the guitar-shaped pond in Encino behind the mystical Thriftimart "T." But I'm not alone there, either. Joan Didion invoked the same location in *Play It as It Lays*. Erickson's *Our Ecstatic Days* made LA's improbable lakes the very image of breaking through to the other side. And when my novel's protagonist swoons for lost paradise, he swoons lakeside. He swoons thinking about rounding a certain bend on Mulholland Drive, where time peels away, leaving in its place one of those fenced, forbidden vistas—a cobalt blue reservoir in the lap of a canyon a half-mile across. Wholeness, temptation, and loss, in a single glance. He swoons because alongside the Encino reservoir, the hills seem to stare directly into Utah, and because even when living in LA you long for it a little, as if it can never be your city altogether.

Of course, if you're a writer who depends on staring into Utah from Encino, you get used to some uneven results. What you don't expect is to keep bumping into other writers in their sleeping gowns. You don't expect to keep finishing each other's dreams. In the first short story I ever sold, a young heir to a swimming-pool business gets lost in Death Valley looking for a chapter president of the Lainie Kazan Fan Club. In Block's first book, from about the same time, a young guy stumbles upon a covenly chapter of the Jayne Mansfield Fan Club. In Sherrill's first novel, after a car crash in the desert, a reporter stumbles upon the ghosts of film stars at a hotel pool; in Plascencia's, a lettuce picker has his way with Rita Hayworth.

Stephen Cooper, who wrote the newly reissued biography of John Fante, *Full of Life,* was my graduate professor at Cal State Long Beach, and as I was writing this essay he coined a name for this new school of writing: Southern California Dream Realism. So I talked him into driving with me to the desert. I had two reasons: I wanted to chase the ghost of Fante's protagonist, Arturo Bandini, to the spot where he lost his Mayan Princess, and I wanted to talk about Fante's themes generally.

Every Los Angeles writer at the outskirts of vision feels

a connection to *Ask the Dust,* the 1939 novel that, more than any other, seems to weep over this city's corpse in the ecstasy of possessing it. ("Los Angeles, give me some of you! Los Angeles come to me the way I came to you, my feet over your streets, you pretty town I loved you so much, you sad flower in the sand, you pretty town.")[4] We all are sufferers. We're not sure, exactly, if the intimacy of our suffering will survive the novel's journey to the big screen, to the masses, to the world. But on the page, it's strictly ours.

Cooper's history with *Ask the Dust* is even more proprietary, but it's also personal. "I was seeking to fill that absence that I didn't even consciously know defined me," he says. "And that was the loss of my father. So I would spend my days just mooning around, moving about, like most young writers, haunted by characters, trying to compose them and failing, failing, failing, failing, failing. . . . And then when I came upon *Ask the Dust,* it was a time in my life when I was living with every pore open to possibility."

Living, in other words, like Bandini himself, who finally writes his look-at-me novel, only to hurl it to the sands where his goddess went mad. "He's gotten what he wanted, in terms of having written the book . . . to be on the shelf next to the big guys. But desire is such that it outlives its fulfillment. And so he must desire something else. . . . It turns to dust, doesn't it, the fulfillment of desire. So getting what

---

4. Claremont McKenna professor Jay Martin has pointed out that what W. H. Auden called "West's Disease"—an LA collision of foolishness, desire, and illusion named after Nathanael West—could just as well have been named after Fante.

you want is, if you will, just a beginning of the eternal and unattainable story of desire."

The ethnic tension between Fante's lovers (an Italian and a Latina) was exquisite too, and Fante tried to turn up the heat under the LA melting pot in an unfinished novel titled *The Little Brown Brothers,* full of romantic impossibility in, among other places, a Wilmington cannery. But editors, Cooper says, misread the work as racist, and it was shelved.

"So we don't know how he would have worked this out. John knew how to cuss people out, but everything he wrote proves that he was doing his best to negotiate this core aspect of our culture. In fact, the only person I ever showed *The Little Brown Brothers* to—because I'm such a Boy Scout about all this—is Philippe Garnier, who translated *Ask the Dust* into French. And Philippe said, 'Oh, thees must be published!'

"Now I'm thinking," Cooper proposes, "what if X number of your visionary writers—I'm just riffing now—but what if Steve Erickson read these hundred pages? What if, name your 10 writers, they could respond however they wanted to? What if sixty years later, a group of writers read this and—not to finish it, but to take up the vision however they wanted to?"

I ask if the tensions in the book still read fresh today.

"Well, yeah. As fresh as they will remain until the republic is a cinder."

When we park Joshua Tree is disarmingly still. We climb over some boulders from the dawn of time, throw pebbles across a chasm, hear them strike. It's the kind of emptiness, behind the mirage, that makes you forget what you came for, or what people back in the city are writing for—not a bad place, all in all, to hurl a manuscript.

But minutes later, it happens—one of those desert-vision ruptures of reality. Outside a convenience store in Yucca Valley—graveyard to Robert Stone's dying soldier protagonist—beside the monster trucks and SUVs, a half-dozen marines in camouflage lounge atop an armored jeep, materialized but ghostly. They look a little like the plastic troops from *Toy Story*. You can see them with your mind's eye, and you can hit them with a stone; they move in slo-mo through the liquor-deli traffic. It's like the scene in *The Day of the Locust* in which actors in period costumes improbably collide, or the back-lot earthquake in *The Last Tycoon,* with marooned extras, jungle backdrops and schooners interposed "like the torn storybooks of child-hood," or the scene in . . . well, never mind. Robert Stone would have known what to say about it.

For now, though, I'm left, along with my protagonist, still peering into that Sherman Oaks pantry that started me writing. And I don't know if it's the future or the past that pulls me. I don't know if my real home is in the time capsule that LA's early hopes were stowed in or just outside the capsule's door, in the world that has vanished around it.

Maybe Southern California Dream Realism is just the ultimate extension of anybody else's literary mode—a way of seeing life stripped of time's pretense. It's a manner of always seeing the terminal desert from the depths of the paradise dream, or paradise from the stretches of life's dry march.

I do know that in our past, in the dark of that pantry, I see the East Coast. Some remnant of ancestry, a quaint hope of continuity, a proper burial, but gone wrong—Waugh's mortuary. I see how fooled my childhood was by every architectural simulation of history.

But I don't know what happens to a civilization, and a literature, that grows up alongside the constant vision of dust. Does the rest of the country even make sense to us here? Was all this aftermath built in from the start? Even the apocalypse, in Los Angeles, feels like history now, the erasures of paradise barely detectable, the age of visions five minutes from over.

That is one scenario for where LA literature is heading. Then there is Francesca Lia Block's view, which she offers in an unpunctuated e-mail: "life/death magic/reality young/old spirit/body masculine/feminine the walls seem to be dissolving and the worlds blending. . . ." In other words, Paradise Next.

I was stuck in traffic on Olympic Boulevard recently, at the last of sundown, heading east through Century City, and I had one of those feelings you get in a city that you now only visit—a city that is no longer the same place where you grew up. The people were strangers. They seemed wealthier and more cosmopolitan, and multinational, and they suffered and sighed separately in their mostly beautiful cars. The cheap apartments I'd once rented near UCLA now cost fortunes, and the sandlot meridians on Little

Santa Monica Boulevard were landscaped, and everything porous and unfinished about this place—all the sweet neglect that once paid off in untold ways—had been finally built over. I wasn't sure if I would ever live in Los Angeles proper again, and my fear is that eventually no one here will think much about oasis and dust, paradise and exile.

Sherrill e-mails me in 20-point type: "Sadly, post-apocalyptic LA will just have to grow old like everywhere else."

But it's always, somewhere, Los Angeles in the 1940s. That sunset in the rearview mirror, past the traffic jam: the cherry of a cigarette, an oleander red.

And think of the next, next generation. Think of Salvador Plascencia's El Monte—where the culture recedes and the lost things survive: the gangs and lettuce pickers, and the elements of milk and oranges and moths, cracked radiators, pollen and sunburns, and lovemaking and coil mattresses, and a ghost of Rita Hayworth. If you want dreams, go to the city's edges. Go where orphans and outcasts are.

12

Requesting the Toronado

In December 1966, plenty of things were happening to people who did not live in the San Fernando Valley. Those needn't concern anyone.

What mattered about that winter to the Valley itself was hard to see then, but for me, it is very nearly the turning point in a slow evolution that began with bridle trails and ended with the Galleria. Until then the Valley was hipper than it looked, instead of the other way around. Grown-ups knew something about what went on beyond the mountains on four sides and seemed to be having the last laugh on it—they had come from many places, where they had learned many lessons, so that their kids could be from nowhere and suffer nothing. All of which might explain the rather delicate philosophical makeup of a lot of eleven-year-olds who had rejected the Santa Claus idea the first time they heard it, who would not be caught dead singing a Christmas carol, and who were absolutely convinced of the sanctity of a local radio promotion known as KHJ's Christmas Wish.

This was when KHJ was called Boss Radio. My eleven-year-old friends, myself, everyone listened to it. We could count on it the same way other people depended on whatever East Coast commiserations got them through the holiday season. I can't remember the rules, whether you could phone in continually or whether you had to wait for the secret cue—something tells me it was "the sound of the KHJ sleigh bells," though I'm sure this is more faithful to the spirit than to the facts—but the premise was, phone in your Christmas Wish and Boss Radio will deliver.

It was not a time in my life when I was asking a lot of hard questions of commercial concerns. A few that perhaps should have come to mind are: Does Boss Radio *have* to honor my Christmas Wish? If not, has the public been (actionably) misled? And how is it that every lucky winner whose voice I hear played back on the air asks for things like $20 so his family can have its first Christmas turkey since before World War II? It was not sinking in—as I tried to get through, dialing from the fetal position, or the take-cover position—that KHJ might be exercising some discretion over whose Christmas Wishes were meaningful enough to honor on the air. Now I dialed fast, then suddenly slow. I was certain this was a test of skill.

Friends of mine were trying to get through, too. Some of them spread sketchy rumors about how KHJ's Christmas Wish was knocking out switchboards all the way to the Kremlin. (Invariably the Kremlin.) I believed all of it—it was a workable worldview, even if it never really cleared the San Bernardino Mountains. Several days passed. More sympathetic stories. Those needy people sure could dial.

And then, at some point, something seemed to have gone wrong with the busy signal. There wasn't one. I heard a click. I heard a ring. "A merry Christmas," sang the recording, "from Boss Radio." This was my moment, our hour, eleven-year-olds the Valley over. I collected myself, waited for my signal to talk. Then, in my clearest speaking voice, I politely requested an Oldsmobile Toronado.

A few words about the Oldsmobile Toronado. It had front-wheel drive. It had racy lines, especially for something the size of a hearse. More important, it was exactly the kind of thing my mother would never think to buy for herself.

My request was never played back, never honored. (Did I get a consolation record album? I can't remember.) Mom was touched. And it did hit me, finally, that we were comparatively lucky to be where we were on Christmas Day, Toronado or no, which is as close to a loss of innocence as a child of the San Fernando Valley, growing up in an age of almost invincible longing, wants to come. Or that was how it felt in 1966, gazing at the warm face of the San Bernardino Mountains, which simplified things so.

Acknowledgments

Some personal writing has to risk being terrible to be anything, and special thanks are owed these editors and mentors for never flinching at my first drafts: Janet Duckworth, John Homans, James Truman, Bob LaBrasca, Susan Murcko, Gregory Wolfe, Joe Donnelly, Laurie Ochoa, Steve Erickson, Tom Christie, Eric Mankin, Stephen Cooper, and Ray Zepeda. The brave founders of Brown Paper Press, Wendy Thomas Russell and Jennifer Volland, went through the manuscript with an enthusiasm and pride that are assumed to be bygone things today. Sally Dworsky said the book belonged somewhere when I was tempted to feel perhaps too realistic about it. I am also grateful to Gary Commins, Ricardo Avila, and all the other clergy and volunteers at St. Luke's Episcopal Church in Long Beach, just the thought of whom brings inexplicable joy in troubling times.

About the Author

Alan Rifkin grew up in the flatlands of Encino, California, the youngest child of a self-taught proofreader and a (trained) OB-GYN, back in the early days of Kaiser Permanente. He became a freelance writer and proofreader for *LA Weekly* and other magazines, raised children (and is raising more children), and then became a creative writing teacher and tutor in Long Beach. A graduate of UCLA (Political Science) and the MFA Fiction Program at California State University, Long Beach, he is the author of *Signal Hill: Stories* (City Lights) and the coauthor, with We Five's Jerry Burgan, of *Wounds to Bind: A Memoir of the Folk-Rock Revolution* (Rowman & Littlefield).

BROWN
PAPER
PRESS

BROWN PAPER PRESS engages readers on topics of contemporary culture through quality writing and thoughtful design. Unbound by genre, our press delivers socially relevant works that advise, guide, inspire, and amuse. We champion authors with new perspectives, strong voices, and original ideas that just might change the world.

For information about new releases, author events, and special promotions, visit **www.brownpaperpress.com**.

Other books by
Brown Paper Press

Relax, It's Just God: How and Why to Talk to Your Kids About Religion When You're Not Religious

I'm Dyin' Here: A Life in the Paper

CPSIA information can be obtained
at www.ICGtesting.com
Printed in the USA
FSOW01n0419280116
16222FS

9 781941 932049